SERIES EDITOR: LEE J

OSPREY NEW VANGUAR

CHALLEN
MAIN BATTLE TANK
1982-1997

TEXT BY
SIMON DUNSTAN

COLOUR BY
PETER SARSON

OSPREY
MILITARY

ISBN 1 85532 485 7

Military Editor: Iain MacGregor
Design: Alan Hamp

Filmset in Great Britain
Printed through World Print Ltd., Hong Kong

For a catalogue of all books published by Osprey Military please write to:

The Marketing Manager, Consumer Catalogue Department, Osprey Publishing Ltd, Michelin House, 81 Fulham Road, London SW3 6RB

Acknowledgments

Lt Col Nigel Aylwin-Foster RTR, Major-General Patrick Cordingley DSO (retd), Col Charles Delamain (retd), David Fletcher, Christopher F. Foss, Angus Fraser (formerly Scots DG), Piers German (formerly LG), WO2 Ken Gifford QRL, Col John Gillman OBE, S/Sgt Kevin Greenhalgh RTR, HQ RAC Centre, Major Albert Hogg KRH, Major Mick Keats RH, Capt Simon Keymer RTR, Denis Lunn MBE, Sgt Colin McKerrell SCOTS DG, Major (retd) Toby Maddison MC, Lt Col Patrick Marriot QRL, Tim Neate, Capt Will Packard QRL, Public Information Land Command & British Forces Germany, David Rowlands, Cpl Colin Shaw KRH, WO1 Bob Soanes RTR, WO2 Tony Sterling QRL, Col T W Terry OBE, Col (Retd) Mike Vickery OBE, VDS, and, Steve Zaloga.

Artist's Note

Readers may care to note the original paintings from which the colour plates in this book were prepared are available for private sale. All reproduction copyright whatsoever is retained by the publisher. All enquiries should be addressed to:

Peter Sarson, 46 Robert-Louis Stevenson Avenue, Westbourne, Bournemouth, Dorset BH4 8EJ

The publishers regret that they can enter into no correspondence upon this matter.

Editor's note

Readers may wish to read this title in conjunction with the following Osprey titles:

CHALLENGER MAIN BATTLE TANK 1982-1997

DESIGN AND DEVELOPMENT

Tank design is a continuous process and, even before a Main Battle Tank (MBT) enters service, concepts and characteristics for its successor are being explored. By 1970, Chieftain MBT was in widespread service with the British Army and, in the following year, the Imperial Iranian Army ordered 780 Chieftains. Designated Chieftain Mark 3/3(P) while the remainder were Mark 5(P) – the P standing for Persia, these models differed only in detail from those in the British Army and all were delivered by 1977. Further purchases of Chieftain were made by Kuwait and Oman giving Britain a strong tank manufacturing industry throughout the 1970s.

The Arab-Israeli War of 1967 had reaffirmed the importance of the tank on the battlefield and demonstrated that heavy armour in its design was a worthwhile attribute, despite the emergence of hollow or shaped charge infantry weapons and anti-tank guided missiles in ever increasing numbers. Indeed, some pundits were proclaiming the demise of the tank in the face of the alarming penetrative power of hollow charge weapons, known hereafter as HEAT (High Explosive Anti-Tank) which uses chemical energy to burn through armour. As a rule of thumb, contemporary HEAT warheads would penetrate steel armour to a depth four times their cone diameter. Such designs incorporated cones typically of

Three generations of British battle tanks thunder down a track at Bovington, the home of the Royal Armoured Corps during comparative testing by the Armoured Trials and Development Unit in 1982. The evolutionary nature of British tank designs since World War 2 is readily apparent in this photograph with, from left to right, Challenger, Chieftain and Centurion. (Mike Garrard – MOD)

the order of 84mm (3½ inches) capable of penetrating up to 340mm (13 inches) of steel. Soviet weapons of this period were the shoulder-fired RPG-7 with a 73mm (3 inches) warhead and the man-portable, wire-guided Sagger AT-3 (Malyutka) anti-tank missile with a 150mm (6 inches) warhead

and a penetrative power of 600mm (24 inches). With 170 missile launchers and 600 RPG-7s in a typical Soviet motor rifle division, these posed a formidable threat to NATO tanks and any conventional design able to withstand such attack would weigh over 200 tonnes. At the same time, contemporary Soviet tanks such as the T-62 and T-64 had larger main armaments, at 115mm and 125mm respectively, than Western tanks which had standardised on the British L7 105mm gun, except for Chieftain with its 120mm. The Soviets had also pioneered the use of Armour Piercing Fin Stabilized Discarding Sabot (APFSDS) ammunition. This was a highly effective round for killing tanks at the ranges for armoured combat envisaged by Soviet planners.

Faced with such threats, Western designers investigated the properties of different forms of armour with the emphasis on trying to thwart attack from HEAT weapons. During the late '50s and early '60s various experiments had been conducted using steel alloy and ceramic laminates which had proved promising but these were difficult to manufacture and therefore expensive. In Britain Dr Gilbert Harvey, a scientist at the Royal Armament Research and Development Establishment (RARDE) at Chertsey, made an interesting discovery when investigating ways to protect fuel cells inside AFVs. By incorporating honeycomb structures composed of certain materials which were intended to inhibit the explosive nature of the fuel, the effectiveness of HEAT rounds was demonstrably diminished. Further experimentation followed and significant successes were achieved against HEAT attack. A programme ensued which would not only defeat HEAT weapons but be effective also against AP, APDS and HESH projectiles; High Explosive Squash Head

The Imperial Iranian Army was a major user of Chieftain and employed it extensively during the Iran/Iraq War, where it gained a reputation for being able to sustain extensive battle damage. This is a Chieftain Mark 5/3(P) or FV4030/1 which was similar to British Army models but for several improvements such as an automatic gearbox to simplify driver training. (MOD)

The second model in the FV4030 range or Shir Iran 1 (Lion of Persia) featured a revised suspension known as Super Horstmann and a lengthened hull to incorporate the new powerpack comprising the 1200 bhp Rolls Royce engine and David Brown gearbox. With the fall of the Shah of Iran, this model was purchased by the Royal Jordanian Army as Khalid. (MOD)

(HESH) being another type of chemical energy armour defeating round favoured by the British.

After a thorough process of testing and trials, the new composite armour, now known as Chobham, was incorporated in an experimental aluminium tank in 1971 designated FV4211 which was based on Chieftain components; Chobham being the name of the town closest to the Military Vehicles and Engineering Establishment (MVEE), formerly RARDE, where it was developed. The construction of the FV4211 coincided with the outset of the US XM-1 programme and, following Anglo-American agreements on the reciprocal exchange of research, details of Chobham armour were passed to the Americans. Trials in the United States demonstrated the remarkable protection afforded by Chobham armour and it was readily incorporated into the XM-1 prototypes being produced by Chrysler and General Motors.

Indeed, the M-1 Abrams was to be the first tank to be put into full production with Chobham armour because the development of FV4211 was terminated in 1972. This followed a decision taken by the governments of Britain and the Federal Republic of Germany (FRG) to develop a single design known as Future Main Battle Tank (FMBT) to replace Chieftain and Leopard 1 respectively. The concept of standardisation within NATO was much espoused at this time and there were perceived to be attractive economic benefits to be accrued from the sharing of development costs. However, as the abortive US/FRG MBT-70 programme had recently proved, joint tank programmes were fraught with difficulties and so it proved once more. As joint discussions ranged over a wide gamut of options another war erupted in the Middle East in October 1973 and once again the future of the tank was thrown into doubt.

Fighting on a scale unseen since World War 2, heavy casualties both in men and machines were suffered by attackers and defenders alike with many of the Israeli losses being attributed to the widespread use by Arab forces of Sagger anti-tank guided missiles and the profligate

The first tank to carry the revolutionary new protection that came to be known as Chobham armour was the FV4211. Using mainly Chieftain Mark 5 components, it was designed and built in the remarkably short time of ten months and two weeks (the designers had hoped to beat the fastest development cycle of a British tank hitherto; that being Churchill at ten months and one week). The FV4211 was a truly innotative design featuring a welded and fabricated hull and turret shell made of aluminium plate instead of the costly castings for the Chieftain. As these parts constituted only 8 per cent of the total vehicle cost, they were expendable and, during refit, all the other components, once refurbished, such as the powerplant, fire control system and Chobham armour envelope could be installed on another shell. However, such a radical concept was not pursued although its influence on the XM-1 programme was significant.(MOD)

deployment of RPG weapons among their infantry. In fact, less than a tenth of Israeli tanks destroyed in battle had been due to missiles and most of these occurred during the first Israeli counter-attacks against the Egyptian incursion across the Suez Canal when Israeli tank crews employed cavalier tactics without sufficient infantry support. However, this fact did not emerge until long after the war following lengthy analysis of Israeli tank losses. There was no doubt, however, that there had been some serious shortcomings in the Western tanks employed by the Israelis not least of which was their capacity to sustain battle damage and continue fighting; an attribute now termed 'survivability'.

During the October War, the Israeli Army was mainly equipped with American M-48 and M-60 tanks in the Sinai Desert against the Egyptians, while on the Golan Heights against the Syrians and Iraqis it used the British Centurion which had been extensively reworked to accommodate the Continental diesel engine of the M-60 with its dependable performance and reduced fire risks. All these tanks shared the same main armament in the well-proven British designed L7/M68 105mm gun. The nature of the fighting for the Israelis differed dramatically between the defensive battles conducted in the close terrain of the Golan to the offensive operations in the wide open desert of the Sinai with, at the outset of the war, a lack of customary air superiority.

Invidious comparisons have been drawn between the American and British designs but the M-60 did suffer some significant losses with high crew casualties due to two major factors. The first was the use of a hydraulic turret traverse which necessitated high pressure lines in the crew compartment. If these lines were ruptured when the tank was hit, a highly inflammable mist was sprayed around inside the tank causing terrible burns to the crews should it ignite. The second was the practice of stowing ammunition in the turret bustle. Since the majority of hits occurred in the turret, the ammunition was often penetrated resulting in catastrophic fires. These were lessons learned long ago by the British and the Centurion had an electric turret traverse, even though this meant a more cramped turret and slower traverse, and all combustible ammunition was stowed in the hull below the level of the turret; a practice followed by Chieftain.

For these reasons, British designers felt vindicated in their design philosophy. The Germans however were less happy since Leopard 1 shared an ammunition stowage layout and turret traverse system similar to the M-60 but with even less armour protection. A replacement was deemed a priority by the Bundeswehr and it accelerated the development of prototypes of a design that had been formulated following the demise of MBT-70; subsequently to emerge as Leopard 2. However the design study for FMBT continued in Britain and Germany with many interesting and innovative concepts, both conventional and unconventional, being addressed. Eventually the study established the requirement for a conventional four man tank with a turret but no agreement could be reached on the timescale for the

A rare photograph shows one of the Concept Test Rigs devised and trialled during the Anglo-German FMBT (Future Main Battle Tank) programme of the 1970s. The design incorporated several standard Chieftain assemblies such as the Horstmann suspension and the L-60 powerplant although the engine compartment was configured to take either a British or a German powerpack. With Chobham armour protecting the frontal aspect, the semi-fixed 120mm main armament was aimed by slewing the vehicle through a hydraulic steering system; the gun only moving in elevation. Because of its configuration and the nature of the bilateral programme, the vehicle was known as Jagdchieftain. (Colonel John Gillman OBE)

introduction of FMBT nor on the vexed question of work sharing, in particular the division of work to satisfy production orders for foreign customers such as the Iranians. The project was terminated by mutual agreement in 1977.

In the meantime, a further major order for Chieftain had been received from the Imperial Iranian Army (IIA) in December 1974. The contract provided for the supply of 1200 Chieftains of an improved version to be called Shir Iran (Lion of Persia); the Ministry of Defence gave the programme the series designation FV4030. In particular the IIA sought improvements in reliability and power output over the troublesome L-60 engine of Chieftain. The design of a new engine was undertaken by Rolls Royce in conjunction with David Brown Gear Industries for the automatic transmission, combined into a single powerpack assembly. Its proposed configuration however was too large for the existing Chieftain hull so a new vehicle had to be developed to accommodate it.

The design was based on that of FV4211 but with Chobham armour mounted on a steel turret and hull; an L11 120mm main armament with the Improved Fire Control System then being introduced into the British Army and a hydropneumatic suspension system produced by Dunlop. Pending the full development of these features, production continued of a basic Chieftain Mark 5 modified to meet the Iranian specifications with an automatic gearbox, increased mine protection and extra fuel capacity under the designation Mark 5/3(P) or FV4030/1. The first of a batch of 150 was completed in July 1976. Stage two of the FV4030 project was essentially a Chieftain Mark 5/3(P) with a revised rear hull to accommodate the new powerpack. The first three prototypes of FV4030/2 were completed by the beginning of 1977 and it was

The MBT-80 was a tank of conventional configuration with a fully-rotating turret and a four-man crew. The photograph depicts the only remaining example of the MBT-80 programme which is now at the Tank Museum at Bovington. It features an early research turret mounted on a test rig hull. Of particular note is the offset high pressure 120mm rifled gun to allow more room for the gunner and the sophisticated fire control system which was an early example of what is now termed the 'Hunter-Killer' type with panoramic sights and thermal imaging. In the event, MBT-80 was an over-ambitious project which ran seriously over budget and it was cancelled in 1979. (The Tank Museum)

demonstrated to the Iranians in March under the name Shir Iran 1.

Problems with the steering units of the TN-37 transmission delayed volume production of Shir Iran 1 as well as development trials of the full specification Shir Iran 2 or FV4030/3, prototypes of which were running during 1977. Production of Shir 1 (the name had now changed) got underway in 1978, with that of Shir 2 being scheduled to start in April 1979, but the fall of the Shah of Iran precipitated the cancellation of the complete contract in February 1979. Fortunately, the Royal Jordanian Army adopted the FV4030/2 as the Khalid MBT and placed an order for 274 in November of that year with deliveries beginning in 1981.

The final model of FV4030 developed for the Imperial Iranian Army was the Shir Iran 2, subsequently known as Shir 2, which was the first to feature the Hydrogas suspension system. One of the reasons for the demise of the FV4211 and the development of FV4030 was the insistence of the IIA on an all-steel tank, because of the problems of stress corrosion cracking associated with aluminium armour. (MOD)

After the collapse of the Anglo-German FMBT project in 1977, Britain was obliged to seek a new solution to Chieftain's replacement. Consideration was given to the purchase of an MBT from another country; the two foreign contenders being the XM-1 and, ironically, Leopard 2. Both tanks were due to enter service in the next few years and the purchase of either would have much enhanced standardisation within NATO. However, as the in-service date requirement for Chieftain's successor was not until the late '80s, it was felt that both designs would be several years old by then and on this basis neither tank would have fully met the needs of the British Army. Similarly, consideration was given to the purchase of Shir 2, at that time at an advanced stage of design, as it was attractive for political and economic reasons as well as enjoying significant commonality with Chieftain to simplify training. Again, like Leopard 2 and XM-1, Shir 2 was being produced to an earlier technological standard and, despite its use of Chobham armour and other technical advances, it did not meet the longer term operational requirements, particularly in regards to its fire control system.

For these reasons, development began of a new tank project designated MBT-80. Drawing on the Anglo-German programme it was to be a tank of conventional turreted design carrying a four man crew. Concept studies addressed the three fundamental areas of MBT design - firepower, protection and mobility. The choice of a main armament proved to be a particularly difficult one between the German 120mm smooth bore gun or a further development of the well proven British 120mm rifled gun. The latter was chosen because of its perceived advantages of being able to fire a greater variety of ammunition natures. In particular it would be able to fire both fin-stabilised and spin-stabilised ammunition, thus allowing more flexibility in defeating the new types of armour arrays then being introduced as well as provide fire support to the infantry with the superior high explosive capability of the HESH round.

The tank was to be built with Chobham armour but with increased protection against top and bottom attack. As to mobility, the stated requirement was a power-to-weight ratio of approximately 27bhp/t for a vehicle of 55 tonnes which predicated an engine of 1500hp. The choice of engine was narrowed to two options: a 1500hp version of the Rolls Royce CV12 TCA diesel and the Avco Lycoming AGT-1500 gas turbine as fitted in the XM-1 Abrams. There was an influential school of thought that favoured the gas turbine so no final decision had been made when the MBT-80 entered the project definition phase in September 1978 which was to last approximately two years. A decision concerning the powerplant was due in mid-1979 with the project entering full development by 1981. Development prototypes were to appear round about 1983-1984 with a design cut-off date in 1985 followed by definitive development models the following year. The in-service date of MBT-80 remained "in the late '80s".

Even by this timescale it was apparent that the British Army would not field an MBT with Chobham armour until almost 20 years after the appearance of FV4211. However, during 1979 it became evident that MBT-80 was unlikely to enter service until the 1990s and the escalating costs of development were proving considerable. With the Soviet Union producing increasingly capable tanks such as the T-64/72 at the rate of over 2000 a year, a new tank for the British Army became evermore urgent. Accordingly, in September 1979 it was decided to introduce a limited number of FV4030/3 models adapted to suit British Army requirements but without major modifications so as to speed development and production with minimal additional costs. As a result the MBT-80 programme was cancelled but a research programme continued to identify an eventual replacement for Chieftain.

The new tank was to be called Challenger[1] and an order was placed for 243, sufficient to equip four armoured regiments together with training and reserve vehicles. Between 1980 and 1981, seven prototype Challengers were built which underwent extensive trials at MVEE and with the Armoured Trials and Development Unit (ATDU) at Bovington. As part of the accelerated development programme, more than 100,000kms of automotive running were completed to assess the reliability, availability, maintainability and durability aspects, or RAM-D as it was then termed. Initial automotive user trials of two prototypes (V4C1 and V4C2) by ATDU were begun in January 1981 but were soon stopped because of recurring failures of the TN37 gearbox. After modifications, ATDU resumed automotive testing in November with an additional two prototypes (V4C5 and V4C6) in what became known as 'The 7-Pack Trial'.

Throughout 1982 development continued and the problems associated with the clutch design and the hydrostatic steering units were addressed by the two companies involved, David Brown Gear Industries and Commercial Hydraulics. Further automotive trails demonstrated that the hydrogas suspension provided excellent cross-country performance and high reliability. In October 1982 Exercise Challenger Trophy 2 was conducted by ATDU on Salisbury Plain involving four

---

1 The decision to call the new MBT Challenger showed a lack of originality as this name had been previously used for the Heavy Cruiser Tank A30, an indifferent design that saw limited service in the final years of World War 2. Of interest, both tanks share the design limitation of a narrow internal mantlet for the main armament which is not conducive to consistent high accuracy.

prototypes on a four-day battlefield exercise. The tanks performed very well and, although Challenger's nominal top speed is 56kph, it regularly exceeded 70kph across the plain. Challenger was accepted for service with the British Army by the General Staff on 14 December 1982 with certain provisos, namely:-

Proven solutions had to be found for the problems associated with the following aspects of Challenger -

1. Main engine generator drive
2. Neodymium YAG Tank Laser Sight
3. Tools and Test Equipment
4. TN37 Gearbox
5. Fightability
6. No 79 Sight
7. Scale of major assembly spares

The first regiment to be issued with Challenger was The Royal Hussars which received their first one on 12 April 1983.

ABOVE **The first production model Challenger was delivered to the British Army on 16 March 1983 during a ceremony at the Royal Ordnance Factory Leeds. Although this vehicle has the armoured barbette for TOGS on the turret side, TOGS was still under development so this is a Challenger Mark 1. Once TOGS was installed the tank became a Mark 2. (MOD)**

CHALLENGER
TECHNICAL DESCRIPTION

Driver's compartment

Challenger is a logical development of the Chieftain MBT with substantial advances in the areas of armour protection and mobility, the latter being the main deficiency of its predecessor. The layout of Challenger is conventional with the hull of welded construction being sub-divided with the driver's compartment at the front, the turret and fighting compartment placed centrally and the power train at the rear. Access to the driver's position is through a hatch in the glacis plate. The driver reclines when closed down and is provided with an armoured periscope situated behind the hatch. The driver's position is central with linked steering levers to each side. Brake and accelerator pedals are normal and a footrest is positioned under the left foot. The speedometer and main engine switchboard are to the driver's right. Mounted low on the right are the GUE (Generator Unit Engine) and emergency gear controls (both difficult to get to when closed down) and, to their rear, the gear selector which operates in a gate with six gear range positions plus neutral. Two hull batteries are located to the driver's left with

RIGHT **The gunner's position in a Challenger 1 is to the right of the gun breach and forward of the tank commander – note the TOGS viewing screen in the centre of the photograph.**

BOTTOM RIGHT **A view of the commander's position shows the plethora of electronic boxes and gadgets that comprises the fire control and turret systems of Challenger. (QRL)**

LEFT **The first regiment to be equipped with Challenger was The Royal Hussars from April 1983. Challenger has a conventional layout with the driver located centrally in the hull front. The driver and commander are seated on the right hand side of the turret with the loader to the left of the breech. The British Army remains convinced of the efficacy of the four-man crew to sustain the 24-hour battle. (Soldier Magazine)**

projectile racks above. A further two batteries and projectile racks are to his right with a stowage pannier above for the driver's personal equipment. By fully lowering his seat the driver can move rearwards into the fighting compartment.

Fighting compartment

The main armament of Challenger is the well proven L11A5 120mm rifled gun as used on Chieftain. The gun has a semi-automatically operating breech with a fume extractor mid-way along its length. It fires separated ammunition, the charge being contained in a fully combustible bag ignited by a 'Tube Vent Electric'. The projectiles and charges are loaded by hand. The charges are ignited by the electrically fired vent tubes; 14 of which are held in a magazine on the breech ring. Being a rifled gun, a wide range of ammunition can be fired including APDS-T (L15A4); APFSDS-T (L23A1); DS-T (L20A1); HESH (L31A7); HESH practice (L32A5); Smoke WP (L34A2) and Canister (L35A1).

The commander is seated at the right rear of the turret with the gunner forward and slightly below him. The commander has a No.32 cupola with fixed unity periscopes providing all round vision and a No.37 combined day/night sight giving the commander x10 and x1 unity vision by day and x4 vision by night. The cupola can be traversed independently of the turret and a 7.62mm L37A2 is mounted externally which can be cocked, elevated and fired from under armour.

The gunner's main sight is a periscopic Tank Laser Sight No.10 Mark 1 with a magnification of x1 and x10. The laser rangefinder is a Neodmium Yag with an operating range of 300 to 10,000 metres with the distance being displayed in both the gunner's and commander's sights. These are integral with the Computerised Sighting System (CSS). Designed by Marconi Command and Control Systems, the CSS integrates information from the laser rangefinder with that of target movement and vehicle attitude from sensors built into the system and automatically calculates the appropriate lay of the main armament. The gun and turret are then driven to the correct position, the gun being stabilised in both axes. Since Challenger was designed primarily to fight from prepared positions covering designated arcs of fire CSS significantly increases the probability of a first round hit against moving targets, particularly at long ranges. The system also allows the gunner to keep targets under close observation while on the

The first major exercise conducted by The Royal Hussars as a complete regiment with Challenger was Exercise Lionheart near Hildesheim in West Germany in September 1984. It is apparent that this is a Challenger Mark 1 as the stowage of kit on the turret front would obscure the angle of view of the TISH if TOGS was installed. (MOD)

move and then make final adjustments for firing at the short halt, the preferred method of tank engagements in the British Army. The tank is also equipped with the Muzzle Reference System which allows the gunner to check any deviation in the gun barrel alignment with the sights and make adjustments without leaving his position in the tank.

One of the major innovations of Challenger was the introduction of TOGS - Thermal Observation and Gunnery System. The system enables Challenger to detect, track and engage targets with equal facility by day or night and, being completely passive, without betraying its own position. It is also highly effective in adverse weather and battlefield conditions, such as mist and smoke. The TOGS system has two principal elements - the Thermal Surveillance System (TSS) and the Gunnery Sighting System (GSS). The TSS comprises the actual thermal imaging equipment of TOGS which picks out any object that radiates heat against the difference in thermal characteristics of its background. Known as the TISH or Thermal Imager Sensor Head, it is mounted within a servo trunnion unit inside an armoured barbette on the exterior of the tank turret. With a dual field of view, the TISH provides a general surveillance and vehicle navigation facility in wide angle and allows target recognition and gun aiming in the narrow angle. The thermal radiation detected by TISH is converted into electrical signals suitable for presentation once they have passed through the Symbology Processing Unit or SPU (pronounced 'spew') which is the control centre of TOGS. This computer integrates data from multiple sources in the GSS and, in essence, turns what would otherwise be a thermal camera into a gunsight. Positioned adjacent to the gunner's and commander's stations, both Individual Visual Display Units show identical information with graticule, aiming marks and ballistic data generated on the thermal picture for gunnery by either crewman with the commander having an override facility.

Challenger is the first tank in British Army service to be fitted with Chobham armour which gives it excellent protection against HEAT warheads that make up the majority of anti-tank weapons on the battlefield. On Challenger the highest level of protection is provided on the hull and turret fronts, giving immunity against the largest hollow charge projectiles such as the Russian AT-4 Spigot which can penetrate 500mm (20 inches) of conventional steel armour. The armour configuration also gives high protection against kinetic energy rounds. According to US sources, the protection over the frontal arc of both Challenger and the M1A1 Abrams is equivalent to about 1000mm (40 inches) of steel armour. While no Challengers were hit by heavy calibre weapons in the Gulf War, seven M1A1s suffered direct frontal hits from tank guns, mainly from the 125mm main armament of T-72, but no penetrations or crew casualties ensued .

Undoubtedly the most dramatic difference between Challenger and Chieftain is the greatly enhanced mobility and agility despite an overall weight of 60 tonnes. Challenger has an integrated powerpack incorporating the engine, transmission and cooling group in a single assembly which can be removed and replaced in under an hour. The powerpack can also be run up on a trolley outside the vehicle for fault finding and tuning. An auxiliary power unit or GUE, provides electrical power for silent watch operation and to assist in main engine starting.

The main engine is a Perkins Engines (formerly Rolls Royce) Condor V12 TCA diesel engine with a rated power of 895 kw (1200 bhp) at 2300 rpm. Exhaust gas turbocharging and charge air cooling devised by Garret-AiResearch are employed to maximise power output from a capacity of 26.1 litres giving Challenger a power-to-weight ratio of approximately 20 bhp/tonne. The engine is located at the front centre of the powerpack compartment with the transmission bolted directly behind it.

The transmission is the David Brown Vehicle Transmission (formerly David Brown Gear Industries) TN37 epicyclic gearbox which allows gear changes to be made while the gearbox is transmitting power. Four forward and three reverse gears are provided with an automatic controller selecting the optimum gear ratio. Incorporated into the TN37 transmission is the Commercial Hydraulics STN37 steer unit giving a continuously variable output with hydrostatically transmitted power. This provides Challenger with an infinitely variable turning capability including a neutral turn whereby the vehicle revolves about its centre. Similarly, the main brakes which are of an oil immersed multi-plate type are incorporated in the TN37 transmission.

Much of the impressive improvement in the cross-country performance of Challenger is due to the hydrogas suspension system which provides progressive spring characteristics with highly efficient damping and large wheel deflection resulting in a much improved vehicle ride across all types of terrain. The total weight of the suspension system is 25 per cent less than the Horstmann bogie type of Chieftain and maintenance is considerably reduced. Being completely independent of each other, the individual wheel stations are simple to replace; so avoiding the vulnerability and complexity of coupled systems or those using torsion bars which are notoriously difficult to repair following mine damage.

Challenger variants

CRARRV - Challenger Armoured Repair and Recovery Vehicle

During the troop trial conducted by The Royal Hussars in 1983, the Chieftain ARRV proved incapable of supporting Challenger MBT adequately. In 1984, the Ministry of Defence invited tenders for the development and manufacture of an ARRV based on the running gear of Challenger. Competitive bids were submitted by Royal Ordnance Leeds and Vickers Defence Systems (VDS). The latter was awarded a fixed price contract in June 1985 for the production of 30 vehicles. By the use of newly acquired Computer Aided Design facilities and years of experience in the manufacture of Centurion and Chieftain ARVs, Vickers completed the first CRARRV in August 1987 and the remaining five of the pre-production models in December; a remarkably short development cycle by any standards.

After intensive trials lasting for 14 months, the production run of 26 CRARRVs began in 1989 with four of the pre-production models being subsequently refurbished to production standard to complete the initial contract for 30 vehicles. Several features on the pre-production models, such as the cradle to carry a spare CV12 powerpack over the engine decks, had to be sacrificed to meet the weight and height restrictions of bridges in Germany; a spare powerpack now being carried in a Warrior Trailer as required. The CRARRV was accepted for service with the British Army in June 1990 with a planned in-service date of May 1991 but this schedule was to be overtaken by events following the invasion of Kuwait by the Iraqi Army in August 1990.

As its designation implies, the CRARRV can be used both for recovery and repair of MBTs in the field. The vehicle carries an extensive range of repair equipment, including welding and cutting equipment and air tools, as well as an Atlas AK6000 M8 hydraulic crane capable of lifting a complete Challenger powerpack. With its TN54 transmission giving much improved manoeuvrability at low speeds and excellent mobility to keep pace with Challenger formations, CRARRV has proved to be an outstanding vehicle from the outset of its service with the British Army. It is capable of towing AFVs of up to 70 tonnes in weight at speeds of up to 30 kph. A further advantage of CRARRV over other support vehicles is that it has been designed to enable a significant amount of repair to be undertaken on MBTs in the field. Such was its success in the Gulf War that a subsequent order for 50 additional CRARRVs was placed with Vickers Defence Systems, the last of which was delivered in early 1993.

CTT - Challenger Training Tank

In February 1988, the Ministry of Defence placed an order with Vickers Defence Systems for the supply of 17 Challenger Training Tanks. In a fixed price contract valued at £18m, these were the first purpose designed training tanks procured by the British Army. As approximately 60 per cent of the total cost of a modern MBT comprises the turret systems, particularly the fire control system, a specialised training vehicle makes economic sense and such a vehicle has been commonplace in European armies for many years. Delivery of the 17 CTTs was made during 1990 and they entered service in 1991. They are used for driver and maintenance training by both the Royal Armoured Corps and the Royal Electrical and Mechanical Engineers.

There have been several private venture weapons systems mounted on the Challenger hull such as the Marconi Marksman twin 35mm

A Challenger 1 Mark 2 Control Tank of Ajax Squadron, 2 RTR, moves down a track during an exercise in West Germany. The primary lens of the TISH is readily apparent with the TOGS door open. This Challenger is fitted with external fuel tanks at the rear, first trialled in 1987, to augment the tanks' range from their bases to the Inner German Border during times of crisis. (MOD)

anti-aircraft gun turret and the Royal Ordnance GBT 155mm howitzer turret. Future variants of Challenger for the British Army may include a Beach Armoured Recovery Vehicle (BARV) as well as a bridgelayer and combat engineer versions to replace Chieftain AVLB (Armoured Vehicle Launched Bridge) and Chieftain AVRE (Armoured Vehicle Royal Engineers) once Challenger 2 is in widespread service.

CANADIAN ARMY TROPHY 1987

By May 1985, The Royal Hussars were fully equipped with Challenger. Meanwhile, the second armoured regiment to be converted to the new MBT, 2 Royal Tank Regiment (2 RTR), received its first Challenger in late 1984. The next two armoured regiments scheduled to be converted were the 17th/21st Lancers (17/21L) and the Queen's Royal Irish Hussars (QRIH). In June 1984, the Ministry of Defence placed an order for an additional 64 Challengers which was sufficient to equip a fifth armoured regiment in BAOR.

Despite its recent introduction into service there were reservations in certain quarters about Challenger concerning that most important aspect of an MBT – its fire control system which was almost identical to that of Chieftain, itself based on early 1960s technology. Inevitably comparisons were drawn with other MBTs then in full scale service such as the M1 Abrams and Leopard 2. This was confirmed following the Canadian Army Trophy of 1985 or CAT '85. Open to all member nations of NATO in the Central Region, the competition was intended to improve the overall standard of tank gunnery within the alliance. However, over the years, it had assumed the character more of a gladiatorial contest with unhappy connotations of national superiority; notwithstanding the commercial kudos attached to the brand of MBT winning the competition.

Unfortunately for the British Army, The Royal Scots Dragoon Guards mounted in Chieftain came last in the CAT '85 competition. Widely regarded as one of the most proficient armoured regiments within the Royal Armoured Corps, the SCOTS DG were longstanding users of Chieftain and had come second in CAT '83. The result was all the more disappointing as they were firing on home territory at the Hohne Ranges. There were no doubts in the minds of the SCOTS DG where the problems lay and that improvements had to be made to the fire control

1:76 scale side view drawing of a Rhino CRAARV. (Tim Neate)

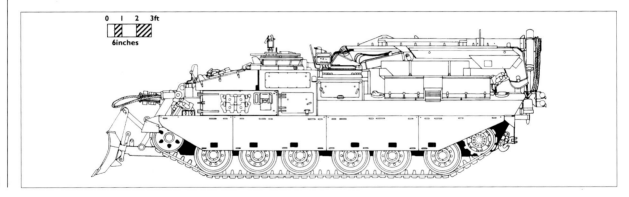

system to improve engagement times as well as providing more extensive technical support for the competition. They also recommended that a regiment be selected as soon as possible for the next CAT and that the crews be drawn from across the regiment rather than a single squadron.

In fact, the latter had been addressed when, based on excellent gunnery results achieved in 1984, 2nd Royal Tank Regiment (2 RTR) was chosen to represent 1(BR) Corps for CAT '87 in time to witness CAT '85. 2 RTR were thus able to lay careful plans that autumn and devise selection procedures to concentrate the necessary talent. Mindful of the implications another disappointing performance would have for the prestige of the British Army and its equipment, the then Chief of the General Staff directed that Challenger be fielded for the next competition. The inherent limitations of Challenger were acknowledged and the overall aim was one of damage limitation in the full knowledge that Challenger could not be expected to win but hopefully would finish among the weaker M1 and Leopard 2 platoons. Throughout 1986, 2 RTR geared gunnery training towards the objectives of CAT '87 and the annual firing in July was used to select competition crews from across the regiment. They were also able to influence timely decisions affecting equipment enhancements deemed necessary for CAT '87 including early procurement of the Improved Computerised Sighting System (ICSS); albeit in prototype form, which in preliminary trials had suggested that engagement times could be halved compared with IFCS.

Following CAT '85, the Committee of Control again tried to eliminate the gladiatorial aspects of the competition and the participating nations were asked to submit proposals to this end. After much discussion and horse trading, a revised set of rules was promulgated in January 1986; however the rules also decreed that each nation must select its entrant from one of two units decided by a random draw held ten weeks before the competition.

This produced a considerable problem for the British Army as its options for the second regiment were strictly limited. Of the 13 armoured regiments, six were equipped with Chieftain which ruled them out while two (17/21L and QRIH) were converting to Challenger

The Challenger Armoured Repair and Recovery Vehicle is manned by members of the Royal Electrical and Mechanical Engineers. It is operated by a crew of three and can carry up to four additional crew or passengers. CRARRV is the first AFV to be developed and manufactured by a private contractor since World War 2. It is also the first to be produced as a fixed-price contract. (MOD)

Camouflaged in the characteristic yellow and green disruptive stripes of OPFOR (Opposing Forces) vehicles, a CRARRV prepares to tow a Chieftain of 1 RTR during Exercise Phantom Bugle on Salisbury Plain in June 1995. CRARRV has a multi-purpose blade which can operate as an earth anchor, dozer blade or stabiliser for the hydraulically-operated crane, with all controls under armour and is equipped with a hydraulically-driven double capstan winch and an independent auxiliary winch. (Tim Neate)

but neither had TOGS, which was considered vital for target acquisition at Grafenwohr with its heated target displays where CAT '87 was to be held. The only other contender was The Royal Hussars who had a squadron fitted with TOGS and had the further advantage of being co-located with 2 RTR. However, The Royal Hussars were committed in 1986 to BATUS in Canada which entailed converting back to Chieftain when they should be training on Challenger/TOGS for CAT.

Meanwhile, 22 Challenger MBTs with TOGS (36KA26-44) were specially prepared to provide each contending squadron with new tanks built to exacting quality assurance standards. These were diverted from the production line resulting in delays to those regiments converting to Challenger. They also incorporated several modifications fitted solely for CAT. Besides the ICSS, these included a finely tuned Tank Laser Sight; a Chase modified loader's firing guard[2]; a less cluttered graticule in the gunner's sight, a revised loading mechanism and an alternative commander's sight with x15 magnification incorporated into a No.21 Cupola – all intended to aid target acquisition and reduce engagement times.

The tanks were fully prepared by the end of October 1986 but because of their autumn commitments neither contending squadron (Badger Squadron of 2 RTR and B Squadron of The Royal Hussars) was able to take up the offer of two days familiarisation on the competition range at Grafenwohr before it was placed in quarantine on 1 January 1987. Severe weather during February and March restricted training further. On the 1 April the final entrant was chosen when The Royal Hussars were drawn out of the hat. Fatefully being the most disadvantaged of the two regiments, the best laid plans made in the wake of CAT '85 were completely undermined.

Following the selection of The Royal Hussars, all training resources were concentrated on B Squadron who set up permanent camp on Battlerun 9 at Hohne. This was laid out to represent the competition range but without any knowledge as to how the targets in the actual competition were to be presented. With increasing familiarity with the complexities of ICSS, some respectable results were achieved. Thus, when crews deployed to Grafenwohr for a 'mini-CAT' competition on a

2 Named after the person who designed it – SSgt Charlie Chase of 4th/7th Royal Dragoon Guards, - the Chase Modification automatically closed the gun breech on operating the loader's firing guard which speeded up the loading procedure. Before it was installed the breech had to be closed manually.

The first purpose-built driver training tank for the British Army was completed and delivered by Vickers Defence Systems in 1990. The 17 Challenger Training Tanks or CTT provide realistic yet cost effective driver and maintenance training for both the Royal Armoured Corps and the Royal Electrical and Mechanical Engineers. (Simon Dunstan)

representative range in May, they compared favourably with the eventual American winners in the M1 and the Canadians in the Leopard CA1. It was at this stage that B Squadron, following the example of other teams, enlisted the services of an acclaimed sports psychologist to help prepare the crews for CAT '87. Imperceptibly, the original directive of the CGS of damage limitation was being forgotten. Under the tutelage of the sports psychologist, the ethos of winning became paramount and with it an exclusive elitism emerged among the competition crews who now adopted colourful cravats and badges while messing separately from support personnel. Within a short time, Hohne witnessed the spectacle of British tank crews humming mantras and dropping ping pong balls onto each other's stomachs to enhance inner awareness.

On 5 June, B Squadron of The Royal Hussars deployed from Fallingbostel to Grafenwohr; a distance of some 700 kms. The competition lasted from 15-19 June with each team being required to make three battleruns; one for each troop or platoon. The run consisted of three bounds with firing taking place while static on these and on the move between them. Targets were at ranges between 800 and 2000 metres. A successful engagement depended on individual tank accuracy and the rapid acquisition and allocation of targets. The objective was to hit the maximum number of targets but, with almost equal points being awarded for time of engagement, a very high premium was placed on speed. Each tank carried ten rounds of main armament and 250 rounds of machine gun ammunition. The three tank troop was required to hit 24 targets with main armament and knock down 60 falling plates arranged in groups of ten; for four tank platoons it was 32 targets and 80 falling plates which statistically is marginally more difficult. A theoretical maximum of 22,600 points could be scored by each troop or platoon based upon

1:76 scale side view drawing of a Challenger Training Tank. (Tim Neate)

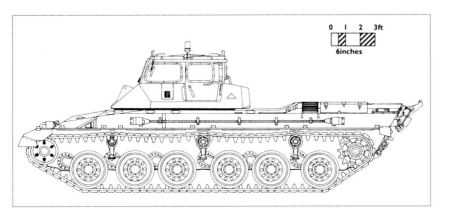

0 1 2 3ft

6inches

the targets hit, the time required and a bonus for unexpended ammunition.

Analysis of the performance of The Royal Hussars during training demonstrated that, in their modified Challengers, crews had the potentiality to achieve 22 hits out of 24 in a mean time of about 14 seconds to achieve scores of between 16,500 and 17,500; exactly what was required for the aim of damage limitation. Once again luck did not favour the British as The Royal Hussars were chosen to fire on the opening run of the competition with no knowledge of the course, whereas all the other teams were allowed to watch and assess the targetry and terrain. Their second run was to be on Wednesday and their third on Friday - the final day of the competition. It was decided that 3rd Troop should open the batting followed by 1st Troop on Wednesday, considered to be the weakest in the squadron, and 2nd Troop, who had shown the strongest performance, on Friday.

In the event, 3rd Troop's first run was entirely consistent with the predictions and, by firing methodically and accurately, 22 out of 24 targets were hit at an average time of 13.64 seconds giving a perfectly satisfactory score of 16,606. However, there had been mechanical problems with the presentation of some of the targets and 3rd Troop were offered a re-run on condition they sacrificed their original score. Having got a feel for the range, the squadron leader believed they could do better on a re-run although it would not take place until late on Wednesday. This meant that in effect 1st Troop was to open the batting which put them under considerable pressure as the Abrams and Leopard 2 teams achieved increasingly impressive scores.

Unfortunately so it proved on the Wednesday when accuracy was sacrificed for speed and, although 1st Troop achieved the fastest average engagement times of the four British runs at 11.7 seconds, seven targets were missed. With the troop communications being broadcast over the public address system, it became apparent that troop control had failed - one commander urging his crew to be faster immediately after a successful three second engagement! With a mediocre score of 14,306 by 1st Troop, 3rd Troop tried to better its performance of Monday but to no avail. Again speed was the enemy of accuracy causing too many errors of lay and only 18 targets were hit as against 22 on their previous run, giving a score of 14,260 - the lowest in the competition so far.

By Friday, The Royal Hussars were lying at the bottom of the score sheet by a wide margin and this was the last opportunity to redeem themselves. 2nd Troop was therefore under

A Challenger 1 Mark 2 of 2nd Royal Tank Regiment moves off on a 'battle run' on the tank gunnery ranges at Hohne during 1989. With a high reputation for gunnery, 2 RTR failed the cut for CAT '87 which was to have far reaching ramifications to the future of Challenger. Here, the L11A5 120mm with its thermal shroud is shown to advantage. (MOD)

intense pressure. All began well but during the move from the first bound disaster struck. The loader in the troop leader's tank, having put a projectile into the breech, had to deal with a broken belt on the coaxial machine gun during firing on the move. Having tried but failed to resolve this problem he returned to the breech when the vent tube magazine fell off. By the time he had fixed this he was confused and loaded a second projectile, jamming the breech - such are the disadvantages of three piece ammunition. Despite hitting 19 targets out of 24, 3rd Troop could only achieve a meagre score of 13,673.

When compared with the winning team's score of 20,490, which incidentally is the highest ever in a CAT competition, the result was dismal. Beside himself with rage, the C-in-C BAOR departed in his helicopter. His entourage followed. By lunchtime, the highest ranking British officer remaining was a subaltern of The Blues and Royals tasked with public relations - not an enviable task in the circumstances. As for The Royal Hussars themselves, they were completely devastated but to their credit none blamed the tank itself. Within weeks, not a single troop leader in the CAT team remained in the British Army.

With its TISH clearly visible, a Challenger 1 Mark 2 kicks up the dust as it advances over the patched prairies at BATUS in Canada. The major shortcoming of TOGS on Challenger 1 is the problem of maintaining precise mechanical alignment of the TISH in its side-mounted barbette with the main armament. It is apparent how the vehicle's callsign on the side plates becomes totally obscured in such conditions. (MOD)

Percentage of Rounds that were Hits by Vehicle Type

	M1	LEO 2	LEO 1	M60	CHIEF/CHALLENGER
1985	75.66	70.89	64.86	62.5	61.04
1987	94.00	92.00	85.00	NA	75.00

Average Kill Times by Vehicle Type

	M1	LEO 2	LEO 1	M60	CHIEF/CHALLENGER
1985	10.23	11.93	16.22	14.10	13.00
1987	9.10	9.60	11.10	NA	12.61

The table on the previous page shows the relative performance of the contending MBTs at CAT '85 and '87.

These figures, however, do not fully reveal the complete superiority in the competition of those tanks equipped with a commander's panoramic sight and gunner's stabilised sight over those without when firing on the move; Abrams and Leopard 2 being twice as probable to hit a target at 88.5 per cent as against 43.5 per cent for Challenger. The ICSS fitted to the CAT modified Challengers incorporated an Independent Aiming Mark in the gunner's sight which attempted to replicate the effect but was not nearly as efficient as true stabilisation. This and a host of other factors touched on in this account militated against Challenger being able to shine during the CAT competition.

It is a measure of the success of the NATO alliance in maintaining the peace for over 40 years that the Canadian Army Trophy assumed such importance and came to be regarded as a valid operational test. Thankfully, there had been no wars to measure the relative effectiveness of all the current generation of MBTs but no manufacturer was slow to trumpet the success of his product following a CAT competition. The ever escalating cost of military equipments has made foreign sales a necessity in any weapons procurement programme. Despite vigorous sales campaigns in the Middle East in 1983, 1985 and again in 1987, the latter coinciding with CAT '87, there have been no foreign purchases of Challenger.

During the preparations for CAT '87, a total of 6,585 rounds of DS/T 120mm ammunition was expended at a cost of approximately £1.9m ($2.9m). Competition crews each fired in excess of 500 rounds during training which was well beyond the 134 permitted by the rules, but the stakes were high and the cost represents approximately the price of one MBT; money well spent if foreign sales had ensued. As to the rules of the competition, each nation interprets them as they will; whether it be the grizzled gunnery instructor who appears in the turret of a young con-

A Challenger 1 Mark 2 of B Squadron, The Royal Scots Dragoon Guards, surges over an earth rampart on the Sennelager training area in West Germany in 1989. In the same year during Exercise White Rhino, German farmers tried to block the passage of tanks with similar barriers to disrupt military exercises as the Green movement became more prevalent. To 60 tonnes of Challenger at speed they proved to be of little impediment but a year later, in the face of Iraqi defensive berms, the need to protect the lower hull front from short range anti-armour weapons as the tanks negotiated such obstacles led to the introduction of Explosive Reactive Armour on the toe and glacis plate of Challenger. (MOD)

A group of Challenger 1s shelter in a fold in the ground on the wide open prairie at BATUS in Canada - those of 1st Armoured Squadron (white fume extractors and white stripes on rear bazooka plates) are at 'check fire' with their main armaments fully elevated while the one at full depression is checking the Muzzle Bore Sight. In the foreground is a Challenger 1 of 2nd Armoured Squadron which can be identified by the white border around the callsign.
(Media Ops Land Command)

script crew or those who surreptitiously video the targets and layout of the competition range after it has been placed in quarantine in order to reprogramme the tank gunnery simulators for their teams. Be that as it may, no amount of splenetic apologia in the letters column of *The Daily Telegraph* could escape the fact that the complexity and poor ergonomics of the turret system of Challenger led to unsatisfactory human performance on the day.

CHALLENGER TO CHALLENGER 2

At the beginning of 1987, it was still the intention of the British Army to retain a mixed fleet of some 1200 Chieftain and Challenger MBTs until the turn of the century when it was anticipated they would be superseded by yet another Anglo-German collaborative venture which was begun in the early 1980s. This project, known as the 'FMBT 2000', was based on the prospect that both countries would need to replace their current designs at about the same time. Development centred on a new technology tank gun using either solid or liquid propellant, and even more advanced technologies such as an electro-magnetic rail gun were being addressed. However, it became evident that a liquid propellant gun could not be fitted to a tank by the year 2000.

Even before it entered service, the limitations of Challenger's fire control system and the need to modernise its turret systems had been recognised. Accordingly, a series of extensive modifications had been set in hand which was known as CHIP or the Chieftain/Challenger Improvement Programme. The development of a new high pressure 120mm rifled gun, the XL-30, and high performance ammunition, including Depleted Uranium (DU) penetrators, was also progressing under the designation CHARM or Chieftain/Challenger Armament.

With the essential brew of tea to hand, the commander of a Challenger 1 Mark 3 of 2 Troop, B Squadron, The Queen's Royal Hussars, directs his driver to a new fire position during Exercise First Crusade on Salisbury Plain in October 1995. The Mark 3 variant has a revised internal layout and armoured charge bins for greater protection of the two-piece ammunition propellant. As the final production model, 156 Challenger 1 Mark 3s were built with the last deliveries to the British Army being made in 1990. (Simon Dunstan)

Originally both programmes were to be implemented on Chieftain and Challenger, although it was realised that retaining Chieftain into the '90s was increasingly risky in face of the improvements in Soviet tanks. For this reason Chieftain separately underwent an uparmouring programme known as Stillbrew and was fitted with TOGS to give it a true night-fighting capability.

However, the success of the plan for a CHIP/CHARM improved Chieftain to soldier on through the '90s depended on it being replaced by a new tank before the year 2000 but this was now highly unlikely. It was at this stage that Vickers Defence Systems which had recently acquired the former Royal Ordnance factory at Leeds with its excess manufacturing capability offered to build a replacement for Chieftain on the basis of a fixed price contract; the design being essentially the combination of a Challenger hull and automotives with the turret of the Vickers Mark 7 private venture export model MBT. The new model was somewhat confusingly designated Challenger 2 Mark 2.

It was against this background that Challenger shortly afterwards entered CAT '87 when it was seen to perform even worse than Chieftain. Not only was the Royal Armoured Corps (RAC) shown in a poor light but it also raised doubts about its operational efficiency and the efficacy of its equipment. In the immediate aftermath, several senior officers within the RAC tendered their resignations but these were refused pending a detailed analysis of Challenger during CAT '87. A formal inquiry was convened at the RAC Gunnery Wing at Hohne on 9 July which examined every aspect of crew and tank performance. Its report found that there had been many reasons for the failures during CAT '87 including mistaken selection procedures for the competition team; the extensive training commitments for British armoured regiments as against other opposing teams who in most cases trained almost exclusively for CAT for seven months or more; the totally inadequate provision of training simulators and coaching aids; the size of troop with only three tanks proved to

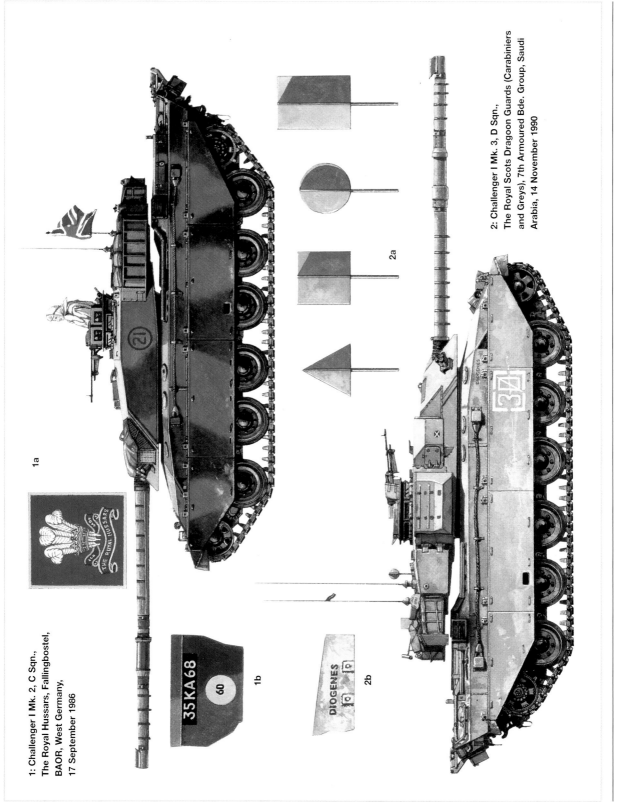

1: Challenger I Mk. 2, C Sqn.,
The Royal Hussars, Fallingbostel,
BAOR, West Germany,
17 September 1986

1a

1b

2a

2b

2: Challenger I Mk. 3, D Sqn.,
The Royal Scots Dragoon Guards (Carabiniers
and Greys), 7th Armoured Bde. Group, Saudi
Arabia, 14 November 1990

35KA68
60

DIOGENES

THE ROYAL HUSSARS

A

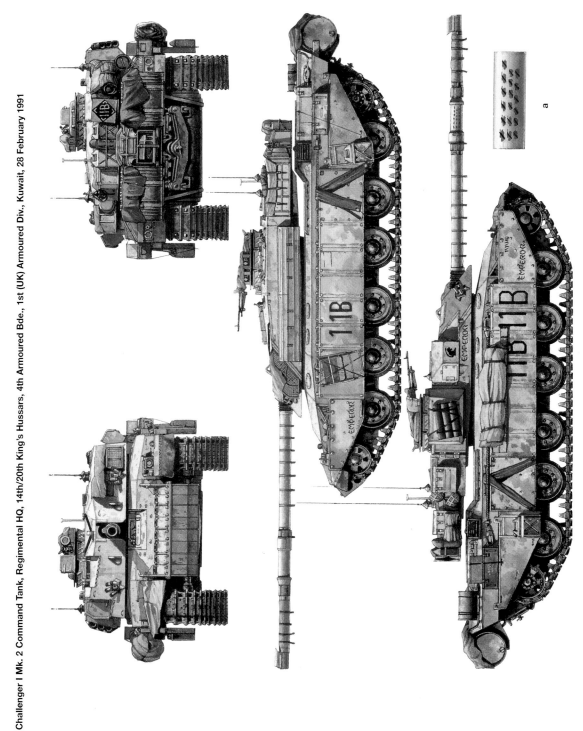

Challenger I Mk. 2 Command Tank, Regimental HQ, 14th/20th King's Hussars, 4th Armoured Bde., 1st (UK) Armoured Div., Kuwait, 28 February 1991

Challenger I Mk. 3, C Sqn., Queen's Royal Irish Hussars, 1 Staffords Battle Group,
7th Armoured Bde., 1st (UK) Armoured Div., Kuwait, 28 February 1991

CMDR C062
SGT. STIRLING
GNR C002
TPR. PLASKITT
OP C034
LCPL. PYKETT
DVR C045
TPR. MARKHAM

a

b

c

CHALLENGER I MK.3
COMMAND TANK, BRIGADE HEADQUARTERS, 7TH ARMOURED BDE, 1ST (UK) ARMOURED DIV, SOUTHERN IRAQ, 26 FEBRUARY 1991

SPECIFICATIONS

Crew: 4 (Commander, loader, gunner and driver)
Weight: Approx 60 tonnes
Length gun forward: 11.55m
Height to top of Commander cupola: 2.88m
Width: Overall 3.52m, over tracks 3.42m
Ground clearance: 0.5m
Ground pressure: At battle weight 0.9KG/cm2
Road speed: Up to approx. 60km/h
Vertical obstacle: 0.9m
Max gradient: 30°
Trench crossing: 3.15m
Shallow fording: 1.07m
Engine: Perkins Condor 12 cylinder 60 V direct injection, 4 stroke diesel, compression-ignition
Capacity: 26.1 litres, rating 1200 BHP (895kW) at 2300 rpm (BSS),11296 BHP (DIN)
Generator: 500 amp
Gearbox: TN37 epicyclic - 4 forward gears, 3 reverse gears, automatic transmission with torque converter
Suspension: Hydrogas type
Main armament: Ordinance breech loading 120mm Tank gun L11A5
Ammunition: Minimum of 44 projectiles consisting of APDS, HESH, SH/Practice, DS/T Smoke, 42 charge containers each holding one APDS or two HESH charges
Coax MG: 7.62mm calibre TKL8A2

KEY

1. D10 communication cable drum
2. Drive sprocket
3. Final drive
4. Main brakes power valve
5. 45-gallon auxiliary fuel drum
6. External tool stowage
7. Gun clamp
8. Transmission covers
9. Radiator
10. Air charge transmission oil cooler
11. Turbo-charger
12. Induction manifold heater
13. Gun depression stop rails
14. Coolant level inspection hatch
15. GUE (auxiliary engine) oil level inspection hatch
16. Main engine
17. TOGS compressor unit
18. Commander's stowage bin (from Ferret Scout Car)
19. TOGS barbette
20. Commander's sight
21. Commander's position
22. GPS Transponder
23. Symbology processing unit ('Spew')
24. Turret services junction box
25. Turret batteries hatch
26. 120mm Gun breech
27. VRC353 Radios
28. 10-Round ready rack
29. NBC control panel
30. 6-Round ready rack
31. L8 7.62mm Coaxial machine-gun
32. Interface box 2 (Radio)
33. Crew box 2 (Radio)
34. Camouflage net stowage basket
35. Smoke grenade dischargers
36. Fire extinguishers
37. Instrument panel
38. Steering levers
39. Handbrake
40. Projectile stowage rack
41. Horn (on side of headlight cluster)
42. Driver's seat (closed down)
43. Gear selector
44. Front lidler
45. MRS mirror shroud
46. Fume extractor
47. L11A5 120mm Main armament
48. Chobham armour side panels
49. Fuel filler cap (2 per side)
50. Transmission heat exchanger

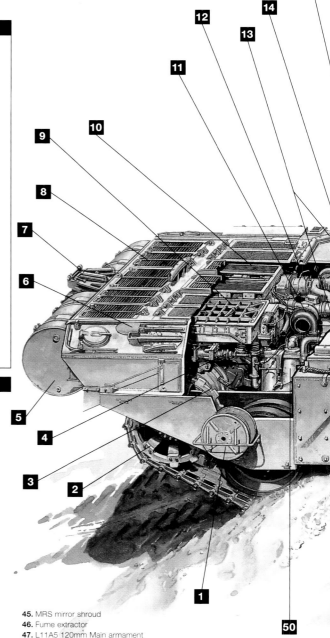

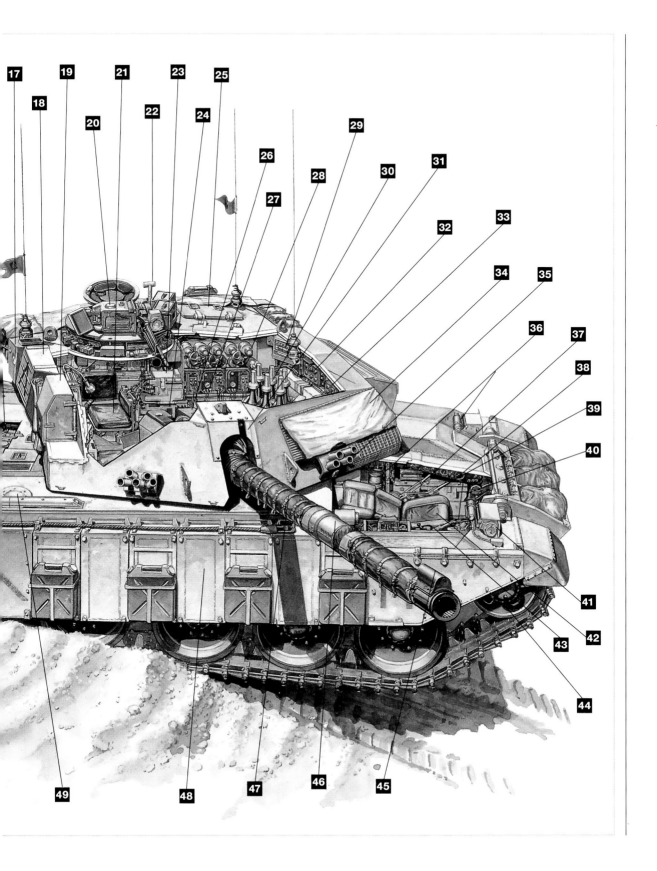

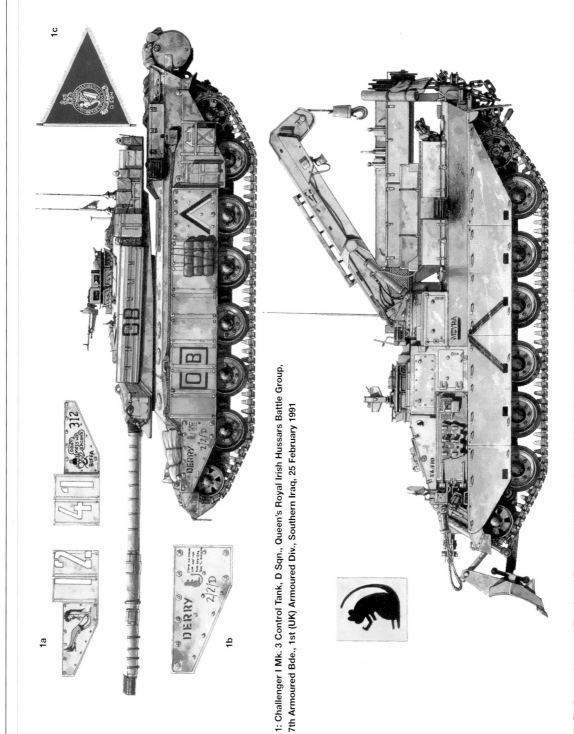

E

1: Challenger I Mk. 3 Control Tank, D Sqn., Queen's Royal Irish Hussars Battle Group,
7th Armoured Bde., 1st (UK) Armoured Div., Southern Iraq, 25 February 1991

2: Challenger Armoured Repair and Recovery Vehicle, 6th Forward Repair Group, Royal Electrical and Mechanical Engineers,
4th Armoured Bde., 1st (UK) Armoured Div., Kuwait, 4 March 1991

Challenger I Mk. 2, 1st Armoured Sqn., The Queen's Royal Lancers, BATUS, Canada, June 1994

F

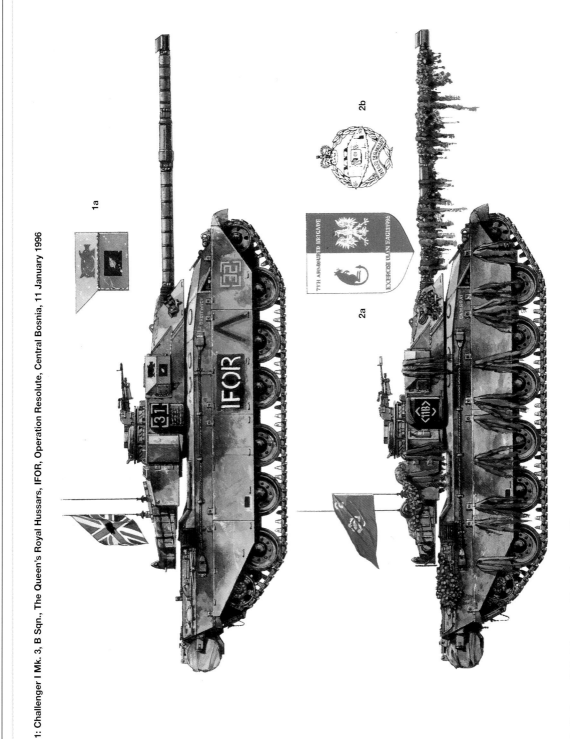

1: Challenger I Mk. 3, B Sqn., The Queen's Royal Hussars, IFOR, Operation Resolute, Central Bosnia, 11 January 1996

2: Challenger I Mk. 2 Command Tank, Command Troop,
HQ Sqn., 2nd RTR, 7th Armoured Bde, 1st (UK) Armoured Div, Poland, 12 September 1996

be disadvantageous psycho-logically and the use of prototype equipment for the competition was deemed to be a mistake, both with the Improved Computerised Sighting System and the x15 magnification commander's sight which compromised observation of the fall of shot. However, most of these were peripheral and the report concluded that the

fundamental cause of the persistently disappointing scores in CAT was the complexity, poor ergonomics and susceptibility to failure of the turret systems of Challenger and Chieftain, compounded by the use of three-piece ammunition leading to human error. This placed British crews under far greater strain than others and imposed an intolerable training load which was exacerbated by the deplorable lack of simulators.

The outcome of the competition was known in the highest political circles and leading questions were being asked about British tank procurement procedures. The concerns in government led to various demonstrations of Challenger together with Abrams and Leopard 2 which proved irrefutably that it was seriously deficient when firing on the move against moving targets. With the prospect of any future main battle tank incorporating advanced technology receding well into the 21st Century, it was decided that a replacement for Chieftain had to be pursued separately and as quickly as possible. Accordingly, a paper was prepared for the Equipment Policy Committee of the Ministry of Defence outlining the options available for a replacement for Chieftain. These included the current Challenger; the Vickers Defence Systems proposed Challenger 2 Mark 2 together with a Mid-Life Improvement Programme for the existing Challenger fleet and two foreign options which were improved versions of the Abrams M1A1 and Leopard 2.

In November 1987, the Equipment Procurement Committee endorsed Staff Requirement (Land) 4026 for the Chieftain replacement programme. This began with a preliminary assessment of the formal proposal by Vickers Defence Systems for its Challenger 2 Mark 2, which for the sake of simplicity the Ministry of Defence called Challenger 2 while the existing MBT became Challenger 1, in comparison with the Abrams

V5 - the fifth Challenger 2 prototype churns through the mud during a demonstration before the Defence Minister of Saudi Arabia on Salisbury Plain in 1993. This model features TECs or Thermal Exhaust Cowls which are a wartime fitting to reduce the tank's thermal signature. (MOD)

In the aftermath of the Gulf War of 1991, Challenger 2 was pre-sented to various Middle Eastern armies leading to the purchase of 18 Challenger 2 MBTs, four CRAAVs and two Driver Training Tanks by Oman in 1993. Below the registration number 06SP95, this Challenger 2 prototype bears the Arabic inscription 'Desert Defender'.(Dennis Lunn MBE)

A production model Challenger 2 is put through its paces by ATDU during acceptance trials at Bovington. The commander has a gyroscopically-stabilised, panoramic sight with an integral laser rangefinder, enabling him to acquire and range targets independently of the gunner. For improved alignment, the TOGS is mounted above the main armament in an armoured housing. (Media Ops Land Command)

M1A1 and Leopard 2 then in-service with their respective armies. Neither of the latter as they existed at the time fully met the British requirements for a Chieftain replacement. However, in the wake of CAT '87, there was considerable dissatisfaction with Challenger, both in the upper reaches of government and within the Royal Armoured Corps. Since doubts had been expressed at the level of armour protection of Leopard 2, a strong faction within the army declared an interest to forego any further delays and procure the Abrams M1A1 which was seen to be a mature and proven design. To others, for the country that invented the tank, the concept of not buying a British tank was unthinkable.

In the event, extensive comparative trials ensued of four contenders for the Chieftain replacement programme – Challenger 2; Abrams M1A2; Leopard 2 (Improved) and the Leclerc – all of which proved to be highly capable with each excelling in one aspect or another while a final decision was to be made by the Equipment Procurement Committee in December 1990.

Once again world events were to impinge on British tank procurement plans. Whereas Challenger was born out of the fall of the Shah of Iran, the collapse of the Warsaw Pact resulted in 'Options for Change' which, under Treasury demands to provide a 'peace dividend', dramatically reduced the number of MBTs to be procured. Initially the intention had been to replace Chieftain on a one-for-one basis and interoperability with the rest of NATO on a purchase of over 500 MBTs was a major factor, with standardisation on the 120mm smooth bore gun being desirable. At this number, the economy of scale favoured the Abrams whereas, on the other hand, co-production of Leopard 2 would allow the British foreign sales to countries denied to the FRG. However, Iran's traditional enemy Iraq had become the focus of world attention following its successful invasion of Kuwait and the deployment of 1st (UK) Armoured Division to the Gulf region deferred any decision until such time as the Gulf War allowed an assessment of the battle performance of Challenger and Abrams.

In the event Challenger went to war and was not found wanting. In no small part this was due to VDS and other major contractors, such as Barr and Stroud; David Brown; Perkins; Marconi; Commercial Hydraulics et al, providing the expertise and support that allowed an availability rate of over 90 per cent to be achieved throughout the campaign. It proved once again that British industry could produce the goods given that the financial restraints imposed by the Treasury were removed for the duration of the war.

In what has been termed 'the only tank battle to be fought on British soil', Vickers Defence Systems were finally awarded a contract at midnight on 28 June 1991 for 127 Challenger 2 MBTs and 13 Driver Training Tanks. This was the minimum number of tanks that was necessary to maintain a viable production line at a rate of approximately 35 tanks per year. With a total value of about £500million ($758m), the contract included an integrated Logistic Support Package whereby VDS was responsible for all aspects of introducing Challenger 2 into service with the first two armoured regiments (Royal Scots Dragoon Guards and 2 RTR) to be equipped with the new MBT.

At the same time, approximately £275million ($415m) was budgeted for a Challenger 1 Mid-Life Improvement Programme which was also to be managed by VDS. Various measures were proposed from rearming Challenger 1 with the L30 high pressure gun to replacing the complete turret with that of Challenger 2. However in the further round of defence cuts known as 'Front Line First', the Ministry of Defence abandoned the plan to upgrade the Challenger 1 fleet and, instead ordered an additional 259 Challenger 2 MBTs from VDS. Furthermore the Royal Armoured Corps was reduced from 13 tank regiments to eight with two in Britain and six in Germany. In turn, each tank regiment was reduced to 38 MBTs as against 50 in the previous organisation, with two at regimental headquarters and three squadrons each with four troops of three tanks. The new composition of the Type 38 organisation was designed to preserve more of the army's famous cavalry regiments in being rather than for any particular tactical considerations. Thus, by the turn of the century, the British Army is scheduled to have a total of 386 Challenger 2 MBTs with 304 in frontline service and the remainder being used for training and war reserves. The Challenger 1 fleet will be disposed of although a number of hulls may be retained and converted to combat engineer vehicles capable of the same degree of mobility as the Challenger 2 MBTs they are required to support.

For export, VDS offers an improved model of Challenger 2 which is named Desert Challenger 2, reflecting its most likely market, or latterly Challenger 2E – the 'E' standing for 'export'. Combining the best elements available, Challenger 2E is less than 50 per cent British, as it comprises German automotives of an MTU 1500 bhp diesel engine and Renk transmission; French sights and a North American fire control system. When built to the British concept of firepower and survivability, this is a truly formidable MBT. (VDS)

Once the 'Quayside Modifications' had been completed, the Challengers of 7th Armoured Brigade Group deployed to the desert to begin training in the area of Al Fadhili - here 2 Troop, A Squadron of The Royal Scots Dragoon Guards manoeuvres at speed during one of the innumerable demonstrations for the world's press in the first weeks following their arrival in the Gulf region. (SCOTS DG)

THE GULF WAR - OPERATION DESERT SABRE

In 1990, following the final deliveries of Challenger, the British Army had a total of 1202 gun tanks in service, comprising 752 Chieftains, 420 Challengers[3], and 30 Centurions AVRE with the Royal Engineers. At this time the Royal Armoured Corps comprised 17 armoured regiments with the seven equipped with Challenger being stationed in Germany with 1st, 3rd and 4th Armoured Divisions of 1st British Corps as one of the four corps of the Northern Army Group within NATO. There were two forms of tank regiments; the Type 57 in armoured brigades and the Type 43 in mechanised brigades. A Type 57 armoured regiment comprised four squadrons, each of four troops of three tanks with two tanks in squadron headquarters and one in regimental headquarters. A Type 43 armoured regiment was similarly organised but with only three squadrons.

Following the Iraqi invasion of Kuwait on 2 August, the British government supported the United Nations coalition forces tasked with responding to such blatant aggression against another sovereign state by deploying 7th Armoured Brigade from Germany to Saudi Arabia. Retaining the title of 'The Desert Rats', the brigade comprised two armoured regiments equipped with Challenger 1, The Royal Scots Dragoon Guards (Carabiniers and Greys) (SCOTS DG) and The

---

3 The Challenger fleet comprises 253 Challenger 1 Mark 2 of which 7 are command variants; 34 control and 212 gun tanks, plus 156 Challenger 1 Mark 3 of which 4 are command, 22 control and 130 gun tanks. The remainder are reworked prototypes used for driver training,s 'pony and trap' models for public display and reference vehicles at various establishments. In addition there are 17 Challenger Training Tanks and 81 'Rhino' CRARRVs.

Queen's Royal Irish Hussars (QRIH), and an armoured infantry battalion, 1st Battalion, The Staffordshire Regiment (1 Staffords) equipped with Warrior. There ensued a hectic period of preparation at Fallingbostel to bring the various units up to wartime establishment. By the end of October, 7th

Armoured Brigade Group had arrived at Al Jubayl on the eastern coast of Saudi Arabia where the brigade came under the operational command of the 1st (US) Marine Division of the 1st Marine Expeditionary Force.

From the outset the decision was taken to equip the tank regiments with the Mark 3 variant of Challenger with its armoured charge bins, for the greater protection they provided to the crews, while the Mark 2s were cannibalised for spare parts. As the tanks arrived in the port of Al Jubayl, they underwent a series of 'Quayside Modifications' to enhance reliability in the desert conditions. These were carried out by REME personnel and an Engineering Support Team composed of engineers from the principal contractors responsible for Challenger including Vickers, Perkins, David Brown, Barr and Stroud and Marconi. Subsequently, the team supported the armoured regiments in the desert by instructing crews in the prescribed procedures for vehicle operation and maintenance.

Once these modifications were complete, the tanks deployed to the desert and training began in earnest in the area of Al Fadhili with gunnery being performed on the Jerboa Range. On 16 November, 7th Armoured Brigade Group was declared operational with the task to prepare for counter-penetration operations in support of 1st Marine Division. In some minds within the US high command, there remained lingering doubts about the efficacy of British equipment, particularly Challenger with its legacy of CAT '87, but these were dispelled after a series of dramatic live-firing exercises on the Devil Dog Dragoon Ranges. As planning began for offensive operations to liberate Kuwait, it was realised that 7th Armoured Brigade Group was likely to be in action in support of the US Marines against heavily fortified defensive positions culminating in fighting in the streets of Kuwait City. Accordingly, the tanks would be facing a gamut of anti-armour weapons at short ranges so it was decided to increase the armour of the Challengers along the hull sides, to protect those areas where the ammunition propellant was stowed in the fighting compartment, and over the hull front to give the driver greater protection. Other modifi-

One of several modifications devised for Challenger during Operation Granby was the installation of a smoke generating system. A pump mounted in a jerry can on the rear hull plate fed diesel from the two reserve fuel drums into the exhaust producing dense white smoke. This was impenetrable to Iraqi observation devices but Challengers could shoot through it using their thermal imaging sights of TOGS. (QRIH)

Once training began in earnest, tank crews soon discovered the problems of operating in the featureless desert. Not least of these was 'sabhka' where the desert sand formed a thin layer over salt marsh beneath with the consistency of wet cement. Once a vehicle broke through the crust it soon became bogged - here three Challengers of B Squadron, SCOTS DG, are being retrieved in the first operational recovery ever undertaken by a CRAARV. (Will Fowler)

cations included extra fuel drums and a smoke generating system which injected diesel fuel directly into the engine exhaust; both of these devices having been used on Soviet tank designs for many years.

Although each tank regiment was supported by Chieftain armoured recovery vehicles, the Challenger Armoured Repair and Recovery Vehicle (CRARRV) was rushed into front line service some seven months before it was due to join the British Army. The first four production models (Faith, Hope, Charity and Big Geordie!) were despatched on 24 September directly from the Vickers factory in Leeds to 7th Armoured Brigade Group in Saudi Arabia. In all, 12 CRARRVs were deployed in support of 1st (UK) Armoured Division. Divided between 4th and 7th Armoured Brigades, they served with the Forward Repair Groups rather than at regimental level. Overall they covered some 19000 kilometres, 7000 kms of which were while towing other AFVs. During the course of the campaign the CRARRVs required five pack changes, giving a mean distance between failures of almost 4000kms which, incidentally, was the original General Staff Requirement for Challenger.

On 22 November, the decision was taken to increase the strength of British ground forces with the addition of 4th Armoured Brigade and other support elements to form 1st (UK) Armoured Division which was transferred from operational control of the Marines to the US Army VII Corps to participate in the major offensive against the Iraqi Army. With two armoured infantry battalions, 1st Battalion, The Royal Scots, and 3rd

1:76 scale side view drawings of a Challenger I Mk. 3, and below, Challenger I Mk.3 (uparmoured). (Tim Neate)

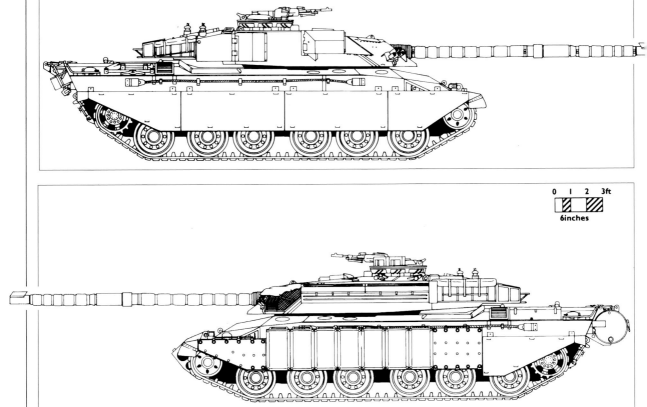

Battalion, The Royal Regiment of Fusiliers, and a single armoured regiment, 4th Armoured Brigade was in fact a mechanised brigade. For this reason, the armoured regiment, 14th/20th King's Hussars, was Type 43, and to bring it up to a wartime establishment of 58 Challengers it was reinforced by A Squadron, The Life Guards, as a complete sub-unit. As many of the regiment's tanks were Mark 2s, new armoured charge bins were designed and fitted in theatre raising them to Mark 2 (ACB) standard; arguably this variant was better protected than the Mark 3 since its armoured bins contained the propellant charges in twos or 'doublets' rather than in the 'triplets' of the Mark 3.

With the armoured door of the TOGS barbette open, a Challenger 1 Mark 3 of The Queen's Royal Irish Hussars displays the full array of supplementary armour fitted to the Challengers of 1st (UK) Armoured Division during Operation Granby, with Chobham armour panels along the sides and Explosive Reactive Armour (ERA) on the glacis plate and toe. (QRIH)

While these protective measures did much to boost the morale of the crews and instil confidence in the survivability of their tanks, enhancements were made to the offensive capabilities of Challenger with the introduction of a highly potent armour-piercing round. Under the codename Jericho, the L26A1 APFSDS round incorporating a depleted uranium penetrator was manufactured by Royal Ordnance as a counter to the T-72M that equipped the Iraqi Republican Guard. With its low silhouette, high speed and powerful main armament of the 125mm D-81 TM (2A46) gun, the T-72M was deemed to be the only serious threat to Challenger on the battlefield. The new round was coupled with an improved propellant charge, the L14A1, which gave both better performance and greater safety. Each Challenger was issued with approximately 12 L26 rounds to be used exclusively against T-72Ms. In the event, no T-72Ms were encountered by 1st (UK) Armoured Division during the war.

However, the two aspects of Challenger that proved to be fundamental to success on the battlefield were TOGS and GPS. The superiority of the Thermal Observation and Gunnery System of Challenger over the sights and night-fighting capabilities of the Soviet tanks that equipped the Iraqi Army was fully appreciated before the war and determined the tactics for tank vs tank engagements. In essence, TOGS allows target acquisition and engagements in open terrain out to 3000 metres - well beyond the capacity of the Iraqis. Accordingly, all engagements were to be at long ranges and, if the enemy closed to within 1500 metres, the Challengers were to fall back to maintain their long range advantage. In the event, the weather was so foul during the conflict and the enemy's tanks were so predominantly static that these tactics were not applicable, although one SCOTS DG Challenger had a successful engagement with a first round hit against an Iraqi tank at

A further modification made to Challengers during Operation Granby was the fitting of two 45-gallon fuel drums at the rear. Here, the crew of a Challenger 1 Mark 3 of B Squadron Royal Scots Dragoon Guards man-handles a fuel drum into the 'upright position' for gravity feed of diesel into the main fuel tanks. This device increased the combat range by some 100 kilometres. (SCOTS DG)

The final preparations are made to a Challenger 1 Mark 3 of the Royal Scots Dragoon Guards in the days just prior to the land offensive. With a Cross of St Andrew on the TOGS barbette, this Challenger belongs to C Squadron whose tanks featured a white painted fume extractor; an identifying feature commonly used at BATUS. Readily apparent behind the commander's cupola is the TOGS indicator which being circular denoted the third troop in the armoured squadrons of SCOTS DG. (SCOTS DG)

4100 metres. The second battle winner was the GPS (Global Positioning System) navigation aid which for the first time in warfare allowed units to determine their exact position with a high degree of confidence, particularly in the featureless desert terrain of southern Iraq. Two types of GPS, Magellan and Trimble, were issued to British units on a typical scale of five per tank squadron. The system was highly efficient as long as sufficient satellites were in alignment for interrogation and it allowed allied forces to manoeuvre freely around known enemy fixed positions and attack from the least expected quarter. At the same time, knowledge of the whereabouts of neighbouring friendly units was a major factor in reducing the incidence of fratricide or 'blue on blue'.

The use of GPS in combination with TOGS gave the battlegroups of 1st (UK) Armoured Division a significant advantage over the enemy as Challengers led repeated day and night attacks with the armoured infantry in their Warriors against a succession of Iraqi brigade sized positions, each objective being codenamed by a particular metal such as Copper, Bronze, Zinc, Steel et al. Within 100 hours the Iraqi Army had been routed by the coalition forces. However, to the trooper in a Challenger tank or the rifleman in the back of a Warrior, having endured weeks of discomfort in the desert and suffered multiple injections against the appalling threat of chemical and biological agents in the certain knowledge that he was facing one of the largest armies in the world which had had many months to prepare defensive positions, all these factors remained an unknown quantity as they crossed the border into Iraq. It is a tribute to the professionalism of the soldiers of the British Army that to a man they faced this prospect without demur and prevailed, while retaining an essential humanity towards the enemy soldiers they fought. Part of this professionalism was an unstated confidence in their equipment, be it Challenger or Warrior, both of which are demanding vehicles to operate but once mastered they have few equals to match them. In the words of Brigadier Patrick Cordingley DSO, Commander 7th Armoured Brigade, "I have always said that Challenger is a tank built for war and not competitions".

Under the leaden skies that were typical throughout the land offensive, a Challenger 1 Mark 3 of A Squadron, 14th/20th King's Hussars, advances at speed. Note the solid black triangle on the forward Chobham armour panel designating A Squadron and the black painted fume extractor which denotes 4th Troop; the other troops each having the requisite number of rings. (MOD)

THE PLATES

A1: CHALLENGER I MK. 2, C Squadron, The Royal Hussars, Fallingbostel, BAOR, West Germany, 17 September 1986 (Sgt. 'Pink' Penkethman)

The Royal Hussars were the first armoured regiment to be equipped with Challenger and this one is finished in the standard British Army camouflage scheme of matt black irregular stripes over the green base colour. It also features low visibility callsigns; in this case 21 within a circle denoting the Troop Sergeant of 2 Troop, C Squadron. The callsign is painted on each turret side and on a plate attached to the turret basket facing to the rear. **1a** The regimental crest of The Royal Hussars adorns the door front of the TOGS barbette. **1b** On the lower hull front is the bridging classification sign of a small black 60 within a solid grey circle, indicating the vehicle's weight in metric tonnes. Above it is the vehicle registration number 35KA68 inscribed in white on a black rectangle. This is repeated on the rear hull plate beside the right hand light cluster, as viewed, with the letter and number groups arranged vertically. Below the towing bar is a white square with the tank callsign and squadron marking superimposed in black, which can be illuminated at night for vehicle identification by personnel on the ground; for instance during night replenishment. This is common to all Challengers and applies to all the colour plates in this book. It also acts as a convoy distance marker at night. On the left rear hull plate above a jerry can is a first aid box indicated by a red cross on a white solid circle. This Challenger is depicted on Battle Run 9 at the Hohne Ranges near Fallingbostel with Prime Minister Margaret Thatcher in the turret and a Union Flag flying from the radio antenna. During a visit with Chancellor Helmut Kohl, she witnessed a firepower demonstration by a squadron of Challengers and a company of Leopard 2s. The two leaders then each climbed aboard one of their nation's respective MBTs and fired one round each at a target down range: both being successful much to the organisers' relief. Following her visit, the PM maintained a keen and inquiring interest in all matters relating to Challenger and the development of its successor.

A2: CHALLENGER I MK. 3, D Squadron, The Royal Scots Dragoon Guards (Carabiniers and Greys), 7th Armoured Brigade Group, Saudi Arabia, 14 November 1990 (Lt. Angus Fraser)

Following several weeks of troop, squadron and regimental training, 7th Armoured Brigade Group was declared operational on 16 November 1990 after a major exercise in the area of Jebel Nufayl. Participating in the FTX, this Challenger 1 Mark 3 belongs to the Troop Leader of 3 Troop, D Squadron, SCOTS DG indicated by the white stencilled callsign on the forward bazooka plate on each side of the tank. The callsign Three Zero is repeated on a metal plate attached to the rear of the turret with the figures and stencilled rectangle painted in yellow on a black background. On the radio antenna is a piece of tape; one of several early measures to identify a troop leader. **2a** Behind the commander's cupola is a TOGS indicator – this one is circular when viewed from any direction. In SCOTS DG, it indicates 3 Troop and is intended to be visible at night through TOGS to aid identification of the various sub-units. Particular to D Squadron is the painting of a white stripe down the middle of the driver's hatch as a reference for the centre line of the vehicle when closed down. Like several young subalterns in the cavalry regiments deployed on Operation Granby, this troop leader was determined to acquire an Arab polo pony and brought his polo sticks just in case, one of which is stowed in the turret basket. In a similar vein the tank, whose registration number is 79KF22, is named DIOMEDES painted in black on the hull sides beside the driver (**2b**) – Diomedes who, in Greek legend, was a hero of the siege of Troy second only to Achilles in bravery or, in the Twelve Labours of Hercules, Diomedes was the king of the Bistones who owned horses which were fed on human flesh. Once vanquished by Hercules, Diomedes was given to his own mares to be eaten which, in the context of the Gulf War, is possibly more appropriate. However, the squadron leader, Major 'Jacko' Page, on attachment from The Parachute Regiment, did not approve of such embellishments and the name did not last beyond the week. Similarly the polo sticks did not survive beyond Concentration Area Keyes.

Although impressive rates of availability were achieved during the Gulf campaign, this has not necessarily been the case in BAOR where the dearth of spare parts and lack of track mileage for MBTs has on occasions reduced the availability of Challenger to less than 20 per cent. This has been exacerbated by the reduction in the number of training areas in Germany which means that many MBTs are confined to their hangars or tank parks. (Simon Dunstan)

'Absolute', a CRARRV of A Squadron, King's Royal Hussars, turns off the 'Panzerstrasse' to be replenished with fuel during an exercise on the Hohne/Bergen ranges in June 1995; lashed to its hull roof is a burnt-out auxiliary engine which it has just removed from a Challenger MBT. The CRARRV is highly regarded by REME personnel who have christened the vehicle 'Rhino' which has been adopted as its official name.(Simon Dunstan)

B: CHALLENGER I MK. 2 Command Tank, Regimental Headquarters, 14th/20th King's Hussars, 4th Armoured Brigade, 1st (UK) Armoured Division, Kuwait, 28 February 1991 (Lt.Col. Mike Vickery)

'EMPEROR' is the traditional name given to the commanding officer's tank of the 14th/20th King's Hussars. It derives from the Battle of Vittoria in 1813 during the Peninsular War when the 14th Regiment of (Light) Dragoons captured the coach of King Joseph Buonaparte as he fled the battlefield. Among the spoils was an item described as 'a silver utensil' which was in fact His Majesty's solid silver chamberpot. This gave rise to the regiment's nickname thereafter of 'The Emperor's Chambermaids', although the contemporary sobriquet is 'The Hawks'. The chamberpot has been preserved ever since in the Officers' Mess and does duty on special occasions as a 'loving cup' with the consumption of copious quantities of champagne. Bearing the registration number 36KA34, EMPEROR was one of only a few Mark 2 Challengers in the Gulf theatre that were not fitted with Armoured Charge Bins before the war began. As the armoured regiment within 4th Armoured Brigade it carries the black jerboa brigade insignia on the TOGS barbette. On all quarters it displays the inverted black V mutual recognition device of the coalition forces and, on the sides and turret rear, the callsign One One Bravo, denoting the commanding officer. Accordingly, the EMPEROR is a command tank with a three-radio fit, including BID for secure clear speech communications with higher headquarters which proved to be of a significant factor in the successful conduct of the fast-moving land offensive. Draped over the top of the turret rear is a fluorescent orange air recognition panel and forward of that is the transponder stalk of the Trimble GPS navigation aid which was such a vital asset in the featureless desert; note the top of the device is painted white. On each forward Chobham armour side panel is the unit code 1/1/HQ - the first figure denotes 4th Armoured Brigade; the second the 14th/20th King's Hussars as the senior regiment within the brigade and finally the sub-unit within that regiment. **A** Painted in red on the fume extractor of the main armament are silhouettes of the enemy vehicles destroyed by the EMPEROR during the 100-Hours War; EMPEROR's contribution to the regimental 'gamebook' being eight T-55s and ten other vehicles including a BRDM-2 which was about to engage the Hawks with Sagger missiles before it was destroyed by One One Bravo.

In January 1996, two armoured squadrons and a headquarters squadron of The Queen's Royal Hussars deployed to Bosnia as part of the British contingent to the NATO Implementation Force or IFOR. DROITWICH, the tank illustrated in Plate G1, heads a column of AFVS through an area of devastation at Mrkonjic Grad in the first patrol conducted by the Challengers of The Queen's Royal Hussars. (Media Ops Land Command)

C: CHALLENGER I MK. 3, C Squadron, Queen's Royal Irish Hussars, 1 Staffords Battle Group, 7th Armoured Brigade, 1st (UK) Armoured Division, Kuwait, 28 February 1991 (Sgt. Tony Stirling)

When the Gulf crisis erupted on 2 August 1990, the QRIH had only recently joined 7th Armoured Brigade in Germany, having been stationed at Tidworth in UK equipped with Chieftain MBT. Accordingly they were new to Challenger and were not scheduled to be fully operational until April 1991. Thus when 7th Armoured Brigade was deployed to the Gulf, the regiment was augmented by a complete squadron of 17th/21st Lancers who had served on Challenger for several years. To benefit from this experience, a formed troop of 17th/21st Lancers was attached to each squadron of the QRIH as their fourth troop. Four One within a circle denotes the Troop Sergeant's tank of 4 Troop, C Squadron. The latter, together with B Squadron, SCOTS DG, were detached from their parent regiments to form the tank element of 1 Staffords Battle Group. Originally named CRAIGAVON on the hull sides beside the driver's position, the name was not reapplied on the Chobham armour side plates. Instead the unit code 2/2/C is painted on the forward Chobham plate; the first 2 denoting 7th Armoured Brigade; the second 2 the QRIH as the second senior regiment within the brigade and C indicating C Squadron. This unit code is repeated on the sides of the rear fuel drums. **A** On each of the second Chobham armour side plates is a zap code with the crew names and their respective functions, a practice peculiar to the QRIH. Behind that is the black chevron and vehicle callsign, both of which are also painted on the rear fuel drums as they are on the turret sides and rear. On the other side of the turret, the callsign Four One within a stencilled circle is painted on the Ferret stowage bin behind the TOGS barbette with the black chevron on the side of the TOGS compressor unit. Behind the commander's cupola is a TOGS indicator which being circular denotes C Squadron; A Squadron being triangular, B Squadron square and D Squadron rectangular, whereas in SCOTS DG the shapes applied to the troops within each squadron. With its registration number 64KG94, this Challenger 1 Mark 3 was commanded by a highly experienced gunnery instructor. Nine targets were engaged during the war of which eight were hit; the one miss being due to a wayward laser rangefinder. One T-55; three MTLBs and a trench system were destroyed. **B** Unwilling to lose their identity as 'The Death or Glory Boys', all the tanks of 17th/21st Lancers carried the regimental motto on the door of the TOGS barbette and, during the final dash to the Kuwait-Basra highway, Four One flew a lancers' flag from the radio antenna.

D: CHALLENGER I MK. 3 Command Tank, Brigade Headquarters, 7th Armoured Brigade, 1st (UK) Armoured Division, Southern Iraq, 26 February 1991 (Brig. Patrick Cordingley)

Effective command and control procedures are fundamental to the successful prosecution of manoeuvre warfare and the commanders of both 4th and 7th Armoured Brigades decided from the outset to direct their respective formations from an MBT during the land battle. 78KF91 is one of four command tanks built to the Mark 3 standard and it served as the mount of Brig. Patrick Cordingley, Commander 7th Armoured Brigade. Its callsign One Four Delta is carried on each hull side as is the black chevron mutual recognition

With the regimental insignia emblazoned on the TOGS door, a Challenger 1 Mk. 3 of 1st The Queen's Dragoon Guards thunders down a road in Central Bosnia during a routine patrol. (Media Ops Land Command)

device of the coalition forces. Along the right hand Chobham armour side plates are four brackets for water jerrycans; but only one is fitted to the other side of the tank on the rear bazooka plate. Tied to the rear central left hand Chobham armour plate is an engine air filter wrapped in CARM (Chemical Agent Resistant Material). Across the ERA (Explosive Reactive Armour) blocks on the lower glacis plate are sandbags which were intended to cover the tank's optical devices when in leaguer to prevent damage from artillery fragments, although they also served to prevent the driver, Cpl. Stavely, from barking his knees on the protruding bolts of the supplementary armour when climbing aboard the tank. On the front turret roof is the black chevron for identification to friendly aircraft with a yellow recognition panel at the rear of the turret. As a command tank, One Four Delta has three radio antennae, two of which carry pennants bearing the Desert Rats' jerboa; the red one was sent to Brig. Cordingley as a Christmas gift from a former Desert Rat who came into possession of it following a parade by 7th Armoured Division to mark the Coronation in 1953. The pennant had been flown by successive generals commanding the division from 1942-1953. At that time 7th Armoured Division had 350 tanks which is almost exactly twice that of 1st (UK) Armoured Division in the Gulf of 176. On the side of the TOGS barbette is the castle motif of the 5th Royal Inniskilling Dragoon Guards with whom Brigadier Cordingley undertook his regimental service. To the rear on the TOGS compressor unit is another red jerboa which is forever to be associated with the Desert Rats of 7th Armoured Brigade/ Division, hence One Four Delta and its commander were referred to by the troops as King Rat. The tank, however, was named *Bazoft's Revenge* in recognition of Farzad Bazoft, the journalist on *The Observer* newspaper who was executed by the Saddam Hussein regime for alleged spying. The name was thought up by the loader, L/Cpl. Colin Shaw who applied it to the fume extractor of the main armament with a black marker pen.

A Challenger I Mk. 2, 2nd Royal Tank Regiment, surges through a ford on the Drawsko Pomorski Training Area in Poland during Exercise Ulan Eagle in September 1996. With the denial of many training areas in Germany, Poland has become an important venue for battlegroup exercises in the British Army. (Media Production Centre Germany)

During the course of the land offensive, 7th Armoured Brigade destroyed 76 MBTs, 68 APCs, 18 artillery pieces and captured 3000 POWs. For his outstanding leadership throughout the campaign, Brig. Cordingley was awarded the Distinguished Service Order.

E1: CHALLENGER I MK. 3 Control Tank, D Squadron, Queen's Royal Irish Hussars Battle Group, 7th Armoured Brigade, 1st (UK) Armoured Division, Southern Iraq, 25 February 1991 (Maj. Toby Maddison)

DERRY was the first British tank to move out of the bridgehead created in the Iraqi frontlines by the 1st (US) Infantry Division (Mechanised) – 'The Big Red One'; crossing Phase Line New Jersey to lead the breakout of 7th Armoured Brigade at 1515 hours on 25 February 1991. The obligatory yellow air recognition panel is lashed down over the turret basket with the rectangular shaped TOGS indicator and Trimble GPS transponder stalk showing vertically from the turret roof. The callsign is repeated on the rear fuel drums with zero on the left and B on the right hand one, applied freehand in black paint. **1a** The scrap views show two examples of what was known as 'bin art' which became more prevalent as the date of the land offensive approached – a popular theme being characters from *VIZ* magazine, such as Biffa Bacon, whereas the classic pin-up is a direct response to the 'nose art' applied to Royal Air Force and USAF aircraft in the Gulf War. These two designs appeared on tanks of The Royal Scots Dragoon Guards. The vehicle registration number is 64KG97, visible only on the rear hull plate beside the right hand light cluster. **1b** All the tanks within QRIH were named after towns and villages in Ireland beginning with the squadron letter; the subject vehicle being

DERRY which caused a certain amount of contention among the interdenominational crew. The name is applied on each forward Chobham armour side plate with the crew zap code and the unit code 2/2/D below applied freehand in black paint. The unit code is also painted on the left front mud flap as viewed. Between the vehicle name and the zap code is the red jerboa of the Desert Rats. This also appears on the faces of the rear attachment points for the towing cables on the hull sides and above the right hand rear light cluster. **1c** With a richly embroidered pennant bearing the regimental insignia flying above the turret, Zero Bravo is the mount of the officer commanding D Squadron which was at the forefront of the QRIH Battle Group throughout much of the offensive; the squadron tally in the war being 22 T-55/59; one BMP-1; three MTLB; seven artillery pieces and six trucks. On the forward turret roof is the black chevron mutual recognition device which is repeated on the hull sides and on the rear of the turret basket; the latter being painted on the folded-out cardboard packaging of a 24-hour combat rations box. This and the two black side chevrons have metallic silver tape inserts which were intended to aid recognition through TOGS but they had no appreciable effect. Taped to the turret roof just in front of the commander's primary sight are detector papers which change colour when exposed to particular chemical or biological agents. A further black chevron is painted on the commander's hatch pointing forwards. Welded centrally to the nose of the tank is a metal bracket which acted as a step for the commander who had sustained a serious knee injury playing hockey; a device copied by several crews in the squadron. For his gallantry during the war, Maj. Toby Maddison, commanding D Squadron, was awarded the Military Cross.

E2: CHALLENGER ARMOURED REPAIR AND RECOVERY VEHICLE, 6th Forward Repair Group, Royal Electrical and Mechanical Engineers, 4th Armoured Brigade, 1st (UK) Armoured Division, Kuwait, 4 March 1991

With its ATLAS crane aloft, MOYRA, one of 12 CRARRVs deployed to the Gulf assists in the repair of vehicles soon after the end of the war. The CRARRVs proved highly effective throughout the campaign and, during the actual conflict, were instrumental in towing several casualties to the finish line on the Basra road, on occasion pulling two AFVs at once. The first four CRARRVs, 70KG67-70, CHARITY; BIG GEORDIE!; FAITH and HOPE respectively, were deployed in support of 7th Armoured Brigade. With the committment of 4th Armoured Brigade and the creation of 1st (UK) Armoured Division, further CRAARVs were depatched to the Gulf with MOYRA 70KG71; BIG ALMA 70KG72; CLARA 70KG73 and MABEL 70KG74 assigned to 4th Armoured Brigade and an additional two, FLORENCE (also known as FLOJO) 70KG75 and BERTHA 70KG76, to 7th FRG of 7th Armoured Brigade. A further two, BARNBOW BELLE 70KG79 and BIG TYKE 70KG80, were held in the War Maintenance Reserve. Many of the names are redolent of the North East and Newcastle-upon-Tyne while the district in the city of Leeds where the vehicles were made gave rise to the name BARNBOW BELLE. Others were named after individuals; for instance, BIG ALMA was in recognition of the dynamic lady in the personnel department of Vickers Defence Systems.

F: CHALLENGER I MARK 2, 1st Armoured Squadron, The Queen's Royal Lancers, BATUS, Canada, June 1994 (Capt. Simon Vaughan-Edwards)

The British Army Training Unit Suffield (BATUS) comprises thousands of hectares of Canadian prairie where live firing of all calibres of weapons allows for the most realistic of field training exercises. In common with all British Army vehicles at Suffield, this Challenger is finished in sand yellow with green irregular stripes. The callsign Zero Charlie is painted with white stencils on black rectangles on each forward bazooka plate and turret side. The callsign is repeated on a metal plate attached to the rear of the turret basket. Forward of the callsign on each bazooka plate is the Zap Code 102, again painted in white on black. At BATUS, each vehicle has its own individual number or Zap Code. The vehicle registration number is 35KA89. The white painted fume extractor is an identifying feature of 1st Armoured Squadron, as is the white stripe down the edge of the rear bazooka plate which also acts as a reminder to the infantry that it is unsafe to be further forward of this line in case the tank fires its main armament. The red metal rectangular device at the commander's cupola indicates that the tank is 'at action'; a white circular one denotes that it is not 'at action' and has no live ammunition loaded in any of its weapons. The

callsign Zero Charlie indicates the second-in-command of the armoured squadron and he is further identified, as are troop leaders, by the single tennis ball impaled on the radio aerial; the squadron leader, Zero Bravo, has a radio aerial with two tennis balls - these balls being visible when dust kicked up by the tank obscures the painted callsigns. At the base of the aerial is a rear facing light cluster to aid station keeping at night. Attached to the rear of the turret basket is a metal tube with lights at each end that allows range safety staff to determine in which direction the turret is pointing at night. This tank also carries a fluorescent orange engineer minefield picket stake which is erected on the turret top when the tank is acting in the Intimate Support Troop role to the infantry. On the front of the turret is an inverted V painted in white which is known as the 'forty-fives'. The white V is visible through the commander's sight and is a marker to indicate safe arcs of fire as determined by range safety staff. Depicted during Exercise Gazala at the culmination of The Queen's Royal Lancers' deployment to BATUS in 1994, this Challenger is crewed by B Squadron. Being the mount of the

Showing the flag is an important aspect of peace keeping operations and this is demonstrated to fine effect by a Challenger 1 Mark 3 of Command Troop, Nunshigum Squadron, The Royal Scots Dragoon Guards (Carabiniers and Greys). (Media Ops Land Command)

squadron second-in-command, this is a Challenger Control Tank with a particular fit of VRC353 radios.

G1: CHALLENGER I MK. 3, B Squadron, The Queen's Royal Hussars, IFOR, Operation Resolute, Central Bosnia, 11 January 1996 (Sgt. Potter)

The Queen's Royal Hussars (The Queen's Own and Royal Irish) were formed from the amalgamation of The Queen's Own Hussars and the Queen's Royal Irish Hussars in September 1993. Following the peace agreement initialled in Dayton, Ohio, on 21 November 1995, the North Atlantic Council authorised the Supreme Allied Commander Europe to deploy Enabling Forces into Croatia and Bosnia-Herzegovina. On 5 December, NATO Foreign and Defence Ministers endorsed the deployment of a multi-national military Implementation Force (IFOR) drawn from all the NATO nations and with additional troops from 16 non-NATO countries. Britain's contribution to Operation Joint Endeavour included a detachment of The Queen's Royal Hussars comprising a small headquarters with two Challengers; two squadrons with 12 Challengers each; a Reconnaissance Troop with eight Scimitar CVR(T) and support elements including two reserve Challengers. The subject vehicle is depicted moving into the devastated area of Mrkonjic Grad on 11 January 1996. Flying a Union Flag emblazoned with a black pig, it bears the callsign Three One in yellow on a black background within a yellow stencilled rectangle on metal plates attached to the turret sides and rear, denoting D Squadron which has provided a complete troop to both A and B Squadrons. The stencilled callsign within a square on the forward bazooka plates shows its attachment to B Squadron. Also on the bazooka plates are the black chevron mutual recognition device, redolent of the Gulf War, and the abbreviation IFOR painted in white on a black rectangle which has been wiped clean for higher visibility. **1a** On the door of the TOGS barbette is the regimental insignia of the QRH and on its top face is the black pig motif which is repeated on the lower hull front below the vehicle registration number 65KG35. Below that is the Military Load Classification of a black 70 within a solid grey circle. The black pig device was adopted as a squadron insignia by D Squadron, The Queen's Own Hussars on its formation in 1978 when the regiment was stationed in Detmold, West Germany. During festivities to mark the occasion, a certain Trooper Gould purloined a large black piggy bank from a local savings bank. The beast was then sawn in half and mounted behind the bar at Hobart Barracks. It adorned virtually every vehicle, item of clothing and artefact in the squadron thereafter. On the side of the TOGS barbette is the white fern leaf emblem of New Zealand marking the affiliation of the 3rd Hussars with 2nd New Zealand Division at the battle of El Alamein which was granted by General Lord Freyberg VC as commander of the New Zealand Expeditionary Force in World War 2. All the tanks in the QRH have names, beginning with the squadron letter, painted in black on the hullsides beside the driver's position. Although some tanks have inspirational names such as DESTINY, most recall regimental battle honours such as DETTINGEN, or place names in the regiment's recruiting areas of London, Birmingham, Northern Ireland and the West Midlands. This tank is named after the town of DROITWICH. On the rear mud flaps are high visibility yellow and orange

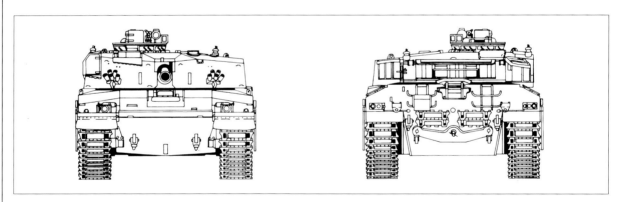

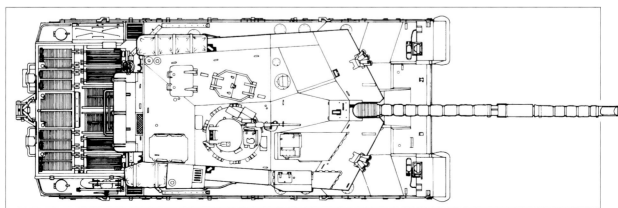

striped hazard markers. Note that the vehicle has a single fuel drum strapped to the rear hull plate on the left hand side (as viewed) which is used for extra stowage of the crew's belongings, usually a butane gas cooker, food and the essentials to brew a cup of tea.

G2: CHALLENGER I MK. 2 Command Tank, 2nd Royal Tank Regiment, 7th Armoured Brigade, 1st (UK) Armoured Division, Exercise Ulan Eagle, Poland, 12 September 1996. (Lt.Col. Nigel Aylwin-Foster)

First and foremost, Challenger was designed for warfare in North West Europe, fighting from successive defensive positions against an armoured onslaught by the Warsaw Pact. Ironically, following the collapse of the latter organisation, NATO battlegroups now undertake field training exercises (FTX) on the territory of their erstwhile adversaries. This Challenger is depicted at the conclusion of maneouvres on the Drawsko Pomorske Training Area during the first FTX to be conducted by the British Army in Poland, (2a) wear the crest shown here was adopted. The vehicle is coated in dust which obscures its basic camouflage scheme of black irregular stripes over the green base colour. The vehicle registration number 34KA91 in white on a black rectangle appears on the lower hull front. Beside it is the Union Flag and below it is the Military Load Classification of 70 tonnes indicated by a black 70 on a solid grey circle. The registration number is repeated on the rear hull plate arranged vertically beside the right rear light cluster, as viewed, below which are diagonal yellow and orange reflective hazard markers. Attached to the jerry cans on the rear of the turret basket is the vehicle callsign One One Bravo within a diamond, both painted in yellow, on a black metal plate. This callsign is also applied to each turret side and signifies the tank of the Commanding Officer. The diamond shape denotes HQ Squadron as is conventional in British armoured regiments. However this is not the case for the other squadrons within the RTR. During the Great War, the original tank units were raised as Companies of the Heavy Machine Gun Corps and then Battalions of the Tank Corps, later the Royal Tank Corps. Subsequently they became Royal Tank

Regiments of which eight survived the contraction of the British Army after World War 2, each corresponding to the originally lettered battalions of the Great War. Since then, their numbers have been reduced to two but with each amalgamation, the traditions of former units have been preserved. Hence, when Options for Change decreed that 1 and 4 RTR, and 2 and 3 RTR be amalgamated, each remaining squadron assumed the designation of former battalions/regiments. Thus, excluding HQ Squadrons, 1 RTR had A, D, G and H Squadrons, and 2 RTR had B, C, E and F, with the shape of the squadron callsign corresponding to A and D in a conventional armoured regiment. For example a circle in 2 RTR signified E Squadron and many of their tanks carried names that adorned those of E Battalion during the Great War. However, following the change of organisation from Type 50 to Type 38 Regiments, further squadrons have been lost with H and F due to be disbanded respectively although, in 2 RTR, some tank names from the original F Battalion/6 RTR have been adopted by the HQ Squadron, which was formerly known as Nero but has now been redesignated as F Squadron. Thus the titles of all four ancestral Machine Gun Corps companies have been retained. Such a sophisticated tribal marking system is bound to confuse other units within the British Army let alone foreign military intelligence. The subject vehicle carries the name CAMBRAI which is arguably the most significant battle in the annals of the RTR. Traditionally the CO 2 RTR's tank has been called NOMAD (as a former CO of 2 RTR, Brig. Christopher Hammerbeck, commander of 4th Armoured Brigade during the Gulf War, carried the name NOMAD on his command tank) and that of CO 3 RTR being CAMBRAI. With the amalgamation of 2 and 3 RTR, the latter has been adopted for the CO and the second tank in RHQ is called NOMAD. It also flies the regimental colours of brown, red and green , which were chosen by Major General Sir Hugh Elles, the original commander of the Tank Corps, (2b) with the regimental badge and motto 'Fear Naught' superimposed. With green always at the top, the colours were first flown in battle at Cambrai on 20 November 1917 and, in the words of that great authority on armoured warfare, Majot General J F C Fuller, aptly signify the role of tanks on the battlefield – 'from mud, though blood, to the green fields beyond'.

LEFT **1:76 scale top front and rear view drawing of a Challenger I Mk. 2. (Tim Neate)**

RIGHT **A Rhino CRARRV of The Royal Scots Dragoon Guards is driven off a Scammell Commander tank transporter in Gornji Vakuf, February 1997. As the successor to IFOR, NATO troops now comprise SFOR or Stabilization Force which in the British Army bears the codename Operation Lodestar. (Media Ops Land Command)**

Notes sur les Planches en Couleur

A1 Les Hussars Royaux furent le premier régiment blindé à être équipé de Challengers, et celui-ci a reçu le camouflage standard de l'armée britannique, qui est constitué de rayures irrégulières en noir mat sur fond vert. Les armoiries régimentaires des Hussars Royaux ornent la porte avant du TOGS en barbette. Ce Challenger est illustré sur la Piste de Combat 9, à la base militaire de Hohne, près de Fallingbostel, avec le Premier Ministre, Margaret Thatcher, dans la tourelle et un drapeau britannique qui flotte à l'antenne radio. **A2** Ce Challenger 1 Mark 3 appartient au Troop Leader de 3 Troop, D Squadron, SCOTS DG, indiqué par le signe d'appel blanc peint au pochoir sur la plaque avant du bazooka, de chaque côté du char. Le signe d'appel Trois Zéro est répété sur une plaque en métal attachée à l'arrière de la tourelle, les chiffres et un rectangle étant peints au pochoir, en jaune, sur fond noir.

B EMPEROR, qui porte le numéro d'immatriculation 36KA34, fut l'un des rares Challenger Mark 2 ayant participé à la Guerre du Golfe à ne pas avoir été équipé de casiers à munitions blindés avant le début de la guerre. Comme il s'agit du régiment blindé de la 4e brigade blindée, il porte l'insigne de la brigade, une gerboise noire, sur le TOGS en barbette. Dans tous les quartiers, on retrouve le signe de reconnaissance mutuelle des forces de la coalition, un V noir renversé, et sur les côtés et à l'arrière de la tourelle, on trouve le signe d'appel One One Bravo qui dénote la présence du commandant.

C Quatre Un à l'intérieur d'un cercle dénote le char du Sergent du 4 Troop, C Squadron. Ce dernier, avec l'escadron B, SCOTS DG, furent détachés de leur régiment parent pour former l'élément chars du Groupe de Combat 1 Staffords. Le code d'unité, 2/2/C est peint sur la plaque Chobham avant, le premier 2 dénotant la 7e Brigade Blindée, le second 2 le QRIH (le second régiment senior de la brigade) et le C indique l'Escadron C.

D 78KF91 est l'un des chars de commandement construits selon la norme Mark 3. Son signe d'appel, One Four Delta, se trouve sur le flanc de chaque châssis, tout comme le chevron noir, signe de reconnaissance mutuel des forces de la coalition. Sur le toit de la tourelle avant, on trouve le chevron noir servant d'identification aux avions alliés, avec un panneau de reconnaissance jaune à l'arrière de la tourelle. Comme il s'agit d'un char de commandement, One Four Delta a trois antennes radio, dont deux portant des fanions sur lesquels on retrouve la gerboise des Desert Rats.

E1 Le panneau jaune de reconnaissance aérienne, obligatoire, est amarré sur le panier de la tourelle, avec l'indicateur TOGS rectangulaire et la tige du transpondeur Trimble GPS qui sortent à la verticale du toit de la tourelle. Le signe d'appel est répété sur les réservoirs de carburant arrières, zéro sur le gauche et B sur le droit, appliqués à la main, à la peinture noire. Le numéro d'immatriculation du véhicule est 64KG97, visible uniquement sur la plaque arrière du châssis, à côté des feux de droite. **E2** Avec sa grue ATLAS en l'air, MOYRA, l'un des 12 CRARRV déployés au Golfe, assiste à la réparation des véhicules peu de temps après la fin de la guerre. Les CRARRV s'avérèrent extrêmement utiles durant cette campagne et, durant le conflit lui-même, jouèrent un grand rôle dans le remorquage de plusieurs véhicules endommagés jusqu'à l'arrivée sur la route de Basra, tirant parfois jusqu'à deux véhicules à la fois.

F Unité d'entraînement de l'armée britannique à Suffield (BATUS), composée de milliers d'hectares de prairie au Canada. Le tir réel d'armes de tous les calibres permet de faire des exercices extrêmement réalistes. Tout comme les autres véhicules de l'armée britannique à Suffield, ce Challenger est peint en jaune sable, avec des rayures vertes irrégulières.

G1 Ce véhicule est illustré alors qu'il traverse la zone dévastée de Mrkonjic Grad le 11 janvier 1996. Il arbore un drapeau britannique orné d'un cochon noir et porte le signe d'appel Trois Un peint en jaune sur fond noir, dans un rectangle jaune peint au pochoir, sur des plaques en métal attachées aux côtés et à l'arrière de la tourelle, ce qui dénote l'escadron D, qui a fourni des troupes complètes aux Escadrons A et B. **G2** Ce Challenger est illustré à la conclusion des manoeuvres dans la zone d'entraînement de Drawsko Pomorske durant le premier FTX réalisé par l'armée britannique en Pologne. Le véhicule est couvert de poussière, qui cache son camouflage de base, constitué par des rayures noires irrégulières sur fond vert.

Farbtafeln

A1 Die Royal Hussars waren das erste Panzerregiment, das mit dem Challenger ausgerüstet wurde. Dieser weist gemäß des standardmäßigen Tarnmusters der britischen Armee eine grüne Grundfarbe auf, über die unregelmäßige Streifen in Mattschwarz aufgetragen wurden. Das Regimentsemblem der Royal Hussars schmückt die Türfassade der TOGS-Lafette. Dieser Challenger ist auf Battle Run 9 im Hohnegebirge in der Nähe von Fallingbostel abgebildet. Die Premierministerin Margaret Thatcher steht im Panzerturm, von der Funkantenne weht die britische Flagge. **A2** Der abgebildete Challenger 1 Mark 3 gehört dem Truppenführer der 3 Troop, D Squadron, SCOTS DG, was durch das schablonierte, weiße Rufzeichen auf der vorderen Panzerfaustplatte auf beiden Seiten des Panzers erkenntlich ist. Das Rufzeichen "Drei Null" taucht ebenso auf einer Metallplatte auf, die auf der Rückseite des Panzerturms angebracht ist, wobei die Zahlen und das schablonierte Rechteck in gelber Farbe auf schwarzem Hintergrund aufgetragen sind.

B Der EMPEROR mit dem Kennzeichen 36KA34 war einer der wenigen Challengers Mark 2 auf dem Kriegsschauplatz im Golf, die vor Kriegsausbruch nicht mit gepanzerten Ladungskästen ausgestattet waren. Wie das Panzerregiment der 4th Armoured Brigade weist er das Brigadeabzeichen mit der schwarzen Wüstenspringmaus auf der TOGS-Lafette auf. Auf allen vier Teilen ist das gegenseitige Erkennungszeichen der Koalitionsmächte aufgetragen, das aus einem umgekehrten schwarzen V besteht. Auf den Seiten und der Rückseite des Panzerturms befindet sich das Rufzeichen "Eins Eins Bravo", das den befehlshabenden Offizier bezeichnet.

C "Vier Eins" innerhalb eines Kreises bezeichnet den Panzer des Truppenfeldwebels der 4 Troop, C Squadron. Letztere Schwadron wurde - wie auch B Squadron, SCOTS DG - vom Mutterregiment abgetrennt, um gemeinsam sie das Panzerelement der 1 Staffords Battle Group zu bilden. Der Einheitskode 2/2/C ist auf der vorderen Chobham-Platte aufgetragen; die erste 2 gibt die 7th Armoured Brigade an; die zweite 2 bezeichnet das QRIH als das zweithöchste Regiment innerhalb der Brigade, und das C steht für C Squadron.

D 78KF91 ist einer von vier Kommandopanzern, die entsprechend dem Standard Mark 3 gebaut wurden. Sein Rufzeichen "Eins Vier Delta" erscheint auf beiden Seiten des Rumpfes, ebenso das gegenseitige Erkennungszeichen der Koalitionsmächte, das aus einem schwarzen Winkel besteht. Auf dem Vorderdach des Panzerturms erscheint der schwarze Winkel, der als Erkennungszeichen für verbündete Flugzeuge dient. Als Kommandopanzer verfügt "Eins Vier Delta" über drei Funkantennen, von denen zwei Stander aufweisen, auf die Wüstenspringmaus der "Wüstenratten" abgebildet ist.

E1 Das obligatorische gelbe Lufterkennungsfeld wurde über den Geschützturm gezurrt, wobei der rechteckige TOGS-Anzeiger und der Stab des Trimble GPS-Sendeempfängers senkrecht aus dem Dach des Panzerturms herausragen. Das Rufzeichen ist auf den rückwärtigen Treibstoffbehältern wiederholt, und zwar die Null auf der linken und das B auf der rechten Seite, von Hand mit schwarzer Farbe aufgetragen. Das Kennzeichen des Fahrzeugs lautet 64KG97, ist jedoch lediglich auf den hinteren Rumpfplatte neben den rechten Scheinwerfern sichtbar. **E2** Mit hochgestelltem ATLAS-Kran ist MOYRA, einer der 12 CRARRVs (Bergepanzer), die im Golf zum Einsatz kamen, kurz nach Kriegsende bei der Reparatur von Fahrzeugen behilflich. Die CRARRVs erwiesen sich beim Feldzug als äußerst nützlich und spielten im Krieg eine wesentliche Rolle beim Abschleppen mehrerer ausgefallener Fahrzeuge zur Schlußlinie auf der Basra-Straße. Einmal schleppten sie sogar zwei AFVs gleichzeitig ab.

F Die British Army Training Unit Suffield (BATUS) umfaßt eine viele tausend Hektar große Fläche kanadischen Graslands, wo Waffen aller Kaliber mit scharfer Munition gefeuert werden, was äußerst wirklichkeitsgetreue Feldübungen ermöglicht. Wie alle Fahrzeuge der britischen Armee in Suffield ist auch dieser Challenger sandgelb gespritzt und weist unregelmäßige grüne Streifen auf.

G1 Dieses Fahrzeug ist abgebildet, wie es am 11. Januar 1996 in die verwüstete Gegend Mrkonjic Grad einfährt. Es weist eine mit einem schwarzen Schwein verzierte britische Flagge auf und trägt das Rufzeichen "Drei Eins" in gelb auf schwarzem Hintergrund innerhalb des schablonierten, gelben Rechtecks aus Metallplatten, die an den Seiten und der Rückseite des Panzerturms angebracht sind. Dieses Zeichen macht den Panzer als der D Squadron zugehörig erkenntlich, einer Schwadron, die sowohl der A als auch der B Squadron eine komplette Truppe zur Verfügung stellte. **G2** Dieser Challenger ist beim Abschluß eines Manövers auf dem Übungsgelände Drawsko Pomorske während der ersten FTX, die die britische Armee in Polen durchführte, abgebildet. Das Fahrzeug ist mit einer Staubschicht überzogen, wodurch das darunterliegende Tarnmuster, das aus unregelmäßigen schwarzen Streifen über der grünen Grundfarbe besteht, schlecht zu sehen ist.